THE PROVIDENCE PALS

MARC

S.T.

DON

KEN

MOLLIE

BOB K.

BOB P.

WILL

STEVE

PETER

JASON

SAM

For Ken.
He would've loved this.

Published by Ulthar Press
700 Metacom Avenue, Warren, RI 02885
http://www.ultharpress.com/

First Edition

Cover illustration by Jason Eckhardt.
Ulthar Press logo by Mike Corley
ISBN: 978-0692495636

THE PROVIDENCE PALS:
MEMORIES AND MISCELLANY

ULTHAR
PRESS

The Outsiders and Others

When I was about twenty years old, I didn't have much direction in life and fewer friends. I was painfully shy, withdrawn and socially inept. This was back in 1982 before the Internet and social media when communication was done largely through phones or letters. I was completely isolated. This all changed when I discovered the work of H.P. Lovecraft.

Through his stories, I would find a new perspective on life and also a new found interest in weird literature and writing. When I was invited to Providence by S.T. Joshi, I became a member of the 'Providence Pals' and nothing was ever the same again.

The 'Providence Pals' were a group of Lovecraftians who had banded together through a mutual love and enjoyment of H.P. Lovecraft's life and stories. Although the group was informal, once you were a member, you were a member for life! We would all get together and discuss Lovecraft and weird fiction and music and life and just generally enjoy each other's company. Through the years, the members included S.T. Joshi, Marc Michaud, Jason Eckhardt, Robert M. Price, Don & Mollie Burleson, Peter Cannon, Steve Mariconda, Will Murray, Robert Knox, Ken Neily and myself.

The group had already begun by the time I came along in 1982 and would flourish for the next decade and a half. Earlier, Marc Michaud had started Necronomicon Press and, together with S.T. Joshi, would begin a campaign of scholarship that would ultimately culminate in Lovecraft finally being regarded as a master of literature. During those years, I would witness many milestones in Lovecraft criticism such as the restoration of Lovecraft's texts to his original, unedited versions and the release of hundreds of Lovecraft's letters and essays that proved he was more than a writer of mere horror but a thinker and philosopher of the highest degree.

It is common to say that, back in the beginning, no one knew who Lovecraft was or what he wrote and that is true. Recognizing a Lovecraftian was an instant impetus to friendship and comradery. We were all fans and enthusiasts in a secret order and, when we walked the streets of Providence, we were keeping Lovecraft's memory alive the best way we could: through reading and sharing. None of us could have dreamed that one day there would be a convention devoted to Lovecraft that would bring thousands of fans from all over the globe or that there would be a "H.P. Lovecraft Memorial Square" in Providence. Back then, there was only the dozen of us, fighting the good fight.

I have been blessed to know these people and to have shared these times with them. I have seen history made before me and, like a knight in Arthur's time, I can say, "I was there!" That experience has shaped me in virtually every aspect of my life.

I owe the members of the "Providence Pals" a debt that I can never fully repay because they accepted a lonely, uncertain lad and made him one of their own. My contributions were never belittled and my opinion was considered as important as any of theirs. To a youth such as I, this welcoming meant more than life itself. I've never forgotten the group or my friends even though time has marched on and miles separate us. When we get together, it is as if the years have only paused and the friendships continue on.

But I wanted to do something to thank all of them for their fellowship over all these years so I decided to compile this book. The members of the "Providence Pals" reads almost like a WHO'S WHO of Lovecraft scholarship. Joshi! Michaud! Eckhardt! Burleson! Mariconda! Cannon! Price! Murray! Knox! Neily! If Lovecraft could construct an All-Star team, he could not draft a better line-up.

So I spread the word far and wide and asked for a contribution from each and, when possible, a short memorial of the group and what it meant to them. What follows are their memories and also some samples of the fine work that each have done in this field. Like knights of old, they flocked to the call and this book is the result.

I would not be the person I am today if not for the "Providence Pals". I would not be a writer. I would not be a publisher. I would not have the interests I do or the friendships I enjoy or the memories I cherish. I would be a lesser man. It's a rare thing to be able to look at an event in one's life and say, "this is where everything changed" but it did for me when I stepped off that train in Providence so many years ago.

This book is a tribute to that time and that place and those people. It is our Golden Road to Samarkand, our path to Randolph Carter's marvelous city of dream, our Xanadu. Although that time and place and these people may pass, the memory shall always remain.

Sadly, one of our number died before this book could become reality and before he could make his own contribution. Ken Neily left us infinitely sadder but profoundly richer and we dedicate this book to his memory and his legacy. I don't think I ever met anyone who was a more passionate fan of Lovecraft and weird literature as Ken and probably never will.

Sam Gafford
Warren, RI
June, 2015

ST JOSHI

"Random Memories of Noreascon II" (1980)

I am not in the habit of writing convention reports, so shall here record merely some random memories of the 38th World Science Fiction Convention in Boston (Aug. 29–Sept. 1) which are of particular interest and note. The majority of my time was spent either in the huckster room, in the cinema rooms, or with the Providence Pals (to which group Crispin Burhham seems to have been added as an honorary member). I did not enjoy this convention as much as I did the 36th World Science Fiction Convention in Phoenix, but nevertheless found much and varied enjoyment.

Vernon Shea, Don Burleson, Marc Michaud, and I held a panel discussion on "Myths about Lovecraft" (a transcript of which may soon appear in *Lovecraftian Ramblings*). The panel was, surprisingly, attended by no less a figure than L. Sprague de Camp, who, as we panelists were filing into the crowded room, attempted to speak to me in Hindi. I, having forgotten that tongue almost completely, merely replied to him, "It's all Sanscrit to me" and proceeded to sit down. De Camp; after the panel, shook the hands of all the panelists and exchanged comments. I later met him again in the huckster room, where he spoke to me in Hindi again; this time I understood, but had to reply in English, for I long ago lost the ability to speak in that or any other of the many Indian dialects. Don Burleson and I repaid his courtesy by attending his own panel on writing the biography of Robert E. Howard. During the course of my talk I managed to attack Darrell Schweitzer, Lin Carter, Stephen King, Arthur Jean Cox, John Taylor Gatto, Philip Shreffler, Ursula Le Guin, Damon Knight (guest of honour at the convention), Isaac Asimov, Brian W. Aldiss, and others—not bad even for me.

I picked up a number of interesting volumes, including two books of Dunsany's plays, Machen's *Things Near and Far* (Knopf ed.) , Wandrei's *Web of Easter Island* and *Strange Harvest,* Long's *In Mayan Splendor,* and even James Hogg's *Confessions of a Justified Sinner.* Both Don Burleson and I wanted to get Wandrei's *Poems for Midnight* (of which several copies were for sale), but all were too expensive for our taste.

The most entertaining event of the convention for me was the night when the Providence Pals, all attempting to sleep in one small hotel room, found themselves curiously unable to get to sleep; at last we ascertained the cause—there was a Bible in the room! After passing it about in disgust amongst ourselves (we attempted to touch it as little as possible), we finally flung it out the window! (The next morning it was gone!—I assumed that some derelict must have picked it up, since no sane person would do so.) We all had wistful plans of buying hundreds or thousands of copies of the paperback *Necronomicon* from Avon and leaving it in all the rooms in the manner of the Gidions. . . .

This convention, it seems to me, had rather fewer fat people than did the Phoenix convention—a point worth noting for those who have read and studied Mr Michaud's "Why I Am Not a Fan." There were some succulent damsels there, particularly in the Masquerade and in the huckster room— indeed, Don B. and I made it a point to pass a particular table as often as we could in order to feast our eyes on one lass who had no compunction in displaying all that could legally be displayed. . . . Unfortunately, the convention was polluted by idiots rigged up in Star Wars or Star Trek outfits, complete with ray-guns and masks—such tedium. . . . Fantasy conventions are actually far saner affairs. The gang has been thinking of dressing up as

8

Cthulhu or a shoggoth, to shew these fools what a real costume is. . . .

The day before leaving for Boston, I met in the John Hay Library a man named John Strysik, who informed me that he had made a movie adaptation (17 min.) of "The Music of Erich Zann," and handed me some publicity information on it. This intrigued me vastly, the more when I learned that the chap was now working on a full-length film version of *The Case of Charles Dexter Ward!* Although time was short, we set an appointment for viewing this film the next day, just before leaving for the convention, at the media services office of Brown University. As a result, Crispin Burhham and I were, the next morning, the first Lovecraftians to see this ABSOLUTELY SPECTACULAR film version of "Erich Zann"—so perfectly faithful to the original (in spite of Zann's playing a violin instead of viol) that I was mesmerised at this miraculous transposition of words upon the screen. Fortunately, Strysik was staying temporarily in Cambridge, and promised to come to the convention on Saturday so that the whole Lovecraftian gang could view the film. This he did, and all the Providence Pals (Crispin, Don Burleson, Marc Michaud, Ken Neily, and others—Vernon was regrettably absent) saw the film at 2.45 a.m. Saturday night (or, rather, Sunday morning). All expressed their profound approbation and enjoyment of the film, and urged Strysik to continue his efforts on the *Charles Dexter Ward* film, which may truly be a landmark in Lovecraftian film adaptation. Strysik also has vaguer plans for a full-length documentary of Lovecraft.

I honestly cannot think of anything more to say. The Lovecraftians attempted to hold a Black Mass (with the intention of summoning Cthulhu from the hotel pool), but were prevented by the hotel security. I regretted the opportunity of not getting to Cambridge and buying classical texts, but such is life. I also regretted not seeing Vernon Shea more than I did, but he was ruled by a tyrannical sister who kept him tied to her apron-strings—here's hoping he'll be more lively in Baltimore! Vernon pestered some dealer into getting my autograph even though the clown hadn't the faintest idea who I was. (At a previous convention I was actually asked for my autograph by no other than Charles Collins—an incident which marks a significant chapter in the Recognition of S. T. Joshi.) I shall probably not be attending the Baltimore convention or any other convention until the Boskone in February 1981—an incalculable loss, I am sure, to the fantasy and science-fiction world.

Some Juvenilia
by S. T. Joshi

1. "Scherzo in D-flat" (1975)

He had long sought that book which would open up awesome vistas of galactic madness, which would hint with monstrous ambiguity at things no man should ever know, which would only half-unveil the curtain of mystery behind which lurked the answers to the very nature and creation of men, and of those things which are not men. . . . Long had he tried to procure that sanity-rocking tome they call *Necronomicon:* and he had not been above using reprehensible means to achieve this end. But it had as yet been in vain, for, try so he might, never could he acquire the book for himself: he could only look on with ill-concealed envy at those who did possess it, in illegible, handwritten manuscripts. But tonight, he had been told, were he to go to the man, he would be given a copy of the unthinkably ancient opus of the mad Arab Abdul Alhazred—and he'd be given it at a price so ludicrously minute that even now he was unsure whether or not it was merely some dastardly joke which his enemies, in acerbic cynicism, had devised.

Come at night, they said he'll give it to you. The address was a little-known and degenerate section of London, where filth and squalor conjoined to produce a decadence vile to the aesthetic mind, filled with the pathetic remnants of humanity who, through their inability to conform or succeed, had been banished here, to dwell wretchedly amongst other loathsome human superfluities in a perpetual rancidity which went far in proving the true elevation of men. The man, unused to such scrofulous examples of humanity, walked with nose wrinkled as if offended by some foetid odour; yet he walked, too, with crisp steps, in the anticipation of the filling at last of his ineffable wish.

He stopped in front of a dilapidated store which aeons ago might have passed for a bookshop. Finding that the barely decipherable number of the store corresponded with the given address, he entered the place, awed that such a slatternly tenement would be the abode wherein his long-desired goal would be consummated.

The man had been waiting for him, and stood now behind a grimy counter with an expression of rank tedium on his face, as if the transaction they would momentarily effect was of the utmost prosiness. The man who had just entered tried to regain his composure, so that he could conclude the affair with at least a modicum of dignity.

"Have you the book?" he asked.

"I do," replied the other, exhibiting a surprising tone of culture and elegance. "Have *you* the money?"

"Yes, of course."

The man handed the other some notes.

"Here you are," said the bookseller, reaching from under the counter and pulling out a volume.

And the man thinks that it was at that very instant that he went mad.

It was a blasphemy of blasphemies; it was something that should not have existed; it was a grotesque mockery of all that was arcane and unfathomable. Such a thing had no place among men: such a thing it was that could only have been produced by the most depraved of modernists. What fiend had perpetrated this vile sacrilege, where the charnel and sepulchral were made to appear the heights of the ludicrously inane? Which mocker of the mystic had conjured up this soul-twisting irony? Was this real, or was it simply a ghastly chimaera spurred by a combination of unhallowed impatience and impalpably inherent masochism? It was all too real.

There it was: the *Necronomicon*—

In paperback.

2. To H. P. Lovecraft (1977)

Death consoles:
You would not care to see
What men have done with your name;
Your work; your spirit; your tardy fame.
You would not care to see
This battered earth, with grinning apes
Whose acts no surprise would cause,
But pain.
Yet you were a cynick:
And Reason found a home—
In both your heart and mind?
Or were you some quaint mystic
Whose foe "Reality" was?
Again:
Were you artist or exorcist?
A gibbering fiend whose true home
Was that empty cell at Sefton?
God! what little minds
Have preyed upon that chipped
Yet awesome monolith of your work!
Without your vision they
Durst pull you down,
That you could cease to gaze upon the stars
And taste the mind that fills *their* mouths and minds.
They would hack and peck;
Remould those runes etched in blood;
For of what other triumphs can they speak?
Giggle in your grave:
And watch these ants on this grain of sand
Smother your page with slimy ichor.
What care you? Your task is done:
You have lit a darkness that now can never dim;
Have built an edifice of marble and gold;
Of porphyry and lapis lazuli
Whose lustre defies alike
The worm and the night.

3. "Fact and Fiction" (1980)

It was hot. The month was only April, but already it was hot. The weather is not kind in Mexico. The paunchy man who was sitting on a chair outside of his tent looked up from the book that he was reading and scanned the bleak expanse of desert. The sneer which their limp black moustaches give to most Spaniards was intensified in this chubby man by the evident distaste with which he carried out his literary task. He had always been vaguely suspicious of books, and thought them either useless or dangerous. It seemed that the present tome fell into the former class.

A youngish man in ragged military dress sauntered to the seated, reading man. Grinning idiotically at him in the way that Spaniards do, he asked:

"Well, what do you think?"

The obese man replied acerbically:

"What do I think? What do I think? I think this is utter nonsense. What is the sense of these babblings about odd foot-prints and toy snakes and invisible monsters and strange hangings? Why can he not write about real things, instead of weird things which never happened? Does he not know that life is not weird?" (Under his breath he murmured that life is but a ridiculous tragedy, but he said it too swiftly for anyone to notice.)

"What should we, then, do with him?" the grinning fool asked.

"Go out and shoot the old one; he has lived too long anyway. And bring me that manuscript he has been working on for the last three months."

The foolish grinner entered a tent where a hideously aged man, hair and moustache totally white and face fantastically wrinkled, was lying on a cot. At the other's entrance the old man said:

"Well, what's the result?"

The fool shook his head slowly.

The old one sighed philosophically, saying:

"Everyone is a critic."

He walked out and stood against a stone wall. The grinning fool loaded a pistol and shot thrice into the old man's head and body.

When he entered the old man's erstwhile tent, he grasped a thick sheaf of papers covered with spidery writing and bore it to the seated obesity.

The latter grinned, lit a match, and began burning, leaf by leaf, the manuscript of Ambrose Bierce's third collection of horror tales.

4. "Life Is *Not* a Hideous Thing" (1982)

It is odd that I, whose published writings on Lovecraft fill more space than his own collected works, have never recorded how I discovered the Master, and how he has shaped and guided my life. I am almost beginning in literal truth to believe that I am a reincarnation of Lovecraft as some have mischievously suggested—or else I feel as if Lovecraft and everything connected with him is a dream or illusion. Was there ever a Lovecraft? Is there an S. T. Joshi? What is anything?

I came upon Lovecraft at the age of thirteen. I was at the time dwelling in the Waste Land of Muncie, Indiana, and by fanatical reading was frantically trying to escape the blight of intellectual stultification so prevalent in the Bible Belt. Most of my fare was detective and horror tales. Browsing through the shelves of the Muncie Public Library, I came across the Arkham House *At the Mountains of Madness and Other Novels.* The title alone would have intrigued me, and I did not let myself be put off by Coye's amateurish cover illustration. But strange to say, when I actually began reading the title story (still my favourite among Lovecraft's works), *I did not like it!*—or rather, I sensed that it was all "over my head," and I found myself unable to follow Lovecraft's rich and convoluted style. (I was a *very* stupid thirteen.) I thus put the volume away (I distinctly recall stopping on p. 53), intending to probe Lovecraft (of whom I had never heard before) at some later time. That time came roughly in the spring of 1972—I was nearly fourteen. This time I began (more sensibly) with *The Dunwich Horror and Others* (Arkham House), and—after being disappointed with the tameness of the first two stories ("In the Vault" and "Pickman's Model")—I thereupon read "The Rats in the Walls" (ugh!), "The Outsider" (whose conclusion I came a hair's-breadth away from guessing), and all the others. I was a Lovecraftian for life.

Elsewhere I have spoken of my nascent attempts at fiction-writing during this period. Although I very quickly became influenced by Lovecraft in my fiction-writing, I wrote comparatively few "Cthulhu Mythos" tales—"The Recurring Doom" (1974) is my longest and last. Ironically, however, I so fell under Lovecraft's sway that I produced many *unconscious plagiarisms* of HPL's tales—and unfortunately I chose his poorest tales to plagiarise. I distinctly recall writing imitations of "The Hound," "Herbert West—Reanimator," "The Statement of Randolph Carter," and the like—all with a complete unawareness of the source of my inspiration. But I soon stopped writing fiction and became devoted to the study of Lovecraft's life and work—from 1975 on this became my prime goal in life. It was de Camp's biography of Lovecraft—discovered at my public library in April 1975—which impelled me to attempt the criticism of Lovecraft, for I was not merely fascinated with Lovecraft's life, but saw that there was much to be done in the study of his work and thought. (I am even now overwhelmed at the thought of how much there is to do in this regard—given time, I could produce a dozen Ph. D. dissertations on Lovecraft without ever leaving my study.)

It was through the de Camp biography, too, that I began to notice rather uneasily how similar to my own were Lovecraft's tastes and attitudes. Here are only a few of the points where HPL and I see eye to eye:

1. We are both Anglophiles.
2. We adore ancient culture (particularly Rome).
3. We loathe the Dark Ages.
4. We are fond of the Enlightenment (although HPL is more lukewarm about the *philosophes*—particularly Voltaire, once my idol—than I, and looks instead to the English).
5. We both adore cats.

15

6. We both enjoy coffee with much sugar (although I am disappointed to say that HPL was not fond of tea, which I prefer to coffee).

7. We were both in our youth shy, reclusive, nervous, and uneasy around strangers.

8. We are both tied to the familiar and dislike the strange and new.

9. We are both (for all practical purposes) atheists (although I detest religion more than he).

But this is becoming comical; it might be easier to enumerate the points where I *differ* from Lovecraft:

1. I (almost shamefacedly) know Greek better than HPl, (I also know Italian and German, which HPL never knew; HPL's Spanish, however rudimentary, is probably better than mine).

2. I like classical music; HPL did not.

3. I have no especial hostility to foreigners—since I am one myself. (But I have become so much the "good European" of Nietzsche that I feel no allegiance to my own country. I am tempted almost to agree with HPL when he said, "The more one thinks about India, the more one wants to vomit.")

There are probably other minor differences, but I can't recall them now. In essence, my outlook and HPL's are the same: his philosophy is mine, his eccentricities and predilections are mine, etc., etc., etc. I must, however, assert that I in truth had many of these attitudes and predilections (however nascent they may have been) *before* ever encountering them in Lovecraft. I have taken up many of his beliefs not because I want to be more like him, but because I am convinced that his beliefs are sensible ones worth taking up.

There was a time, however, when I was approaching fanaticism in this regard: I wanted to read nothing but the books he read, go nowhere but where he went, and do nothing but what he did. Even now I not only try to imitate his style (even in nonfiction), but have also adopted his eccentricities of spelling, grammar, and punctuation. Some of my correspondents now say that even my handwriting looks like HPL's . .

. "I am it and it is I. . . ." I am still almost ashamed that I shall attain a Ph.D. when HPL never got a high-school diploma; and I can see HPL in Hades shrugging his shoulders in disgust when I listen for hours on end to Vivaldi or Handel. . . . Indeed, I am now becoming irritated that HPL did not share some of my attitudes: why did he not keep his nose to the grindstone and learn Greek? Why did he not give music a chance? (Here's another coincidence: both he and I started violin lessons at the age of seven, and both of us quit—although he after two years and I after eleven—because we could not endure practicing. Of course, the strangest and most unnerving coincidence is that Lovecraft's mother and my mother *share the same birthday*. . . . Make of that what you will.) Conversely, I am ashamed that I do not pursue the sciences as he did. I also find myself becoming uncontrollably angry and offended when someone makes a snide reference to HPL.

My whole intellectual life has been shaped by Lovecraft. I would never have learnt Latin had I not wondered why HPL was fond of it; nearly all I know about colonial American history I know from Lovecraft; I discovered Nietzsche, Schopenhauer, Bertrand Russell, George Santayana, and even the Presocratics through Lovecraft. I am now convinced that HPL's letters are his greatest work, and someday I shall publish his Collected Correspondence—if I don't go blind editing his Collected Works.

Of late I have increasingly abandoned Lovecraft for the pursuit of classical and musicological studies—although even now every moment spent away from Lovecraft makes me feel guilty. But I have now returned in full measure to Lovecraftian studies, and I daresay I shall never abandon the field, however little time I will have for it in the future.

Do I regret having fallen so much under the sway of Lovecraft, and not allowing my "own" character to evolve? Not much, since without Lovecraft S. T. Joshi would be the most abysmal little wretch imaginable. It is only when I am studying Lovecraft that I feel justified in amending one of his many resounding utterances and saying, "Life is *not* a hideous thing."

MARC MICHAUD

I wrote this narrative back in 1980, when the "Pals" ventured to the World Fantasy Convention in Baltimore. There was some question about my "editing" it, but I decided to leave the piece as is. I remember there were some comments I made that weren't politically correct then, and am guessing they're even less politically correct 35 years later. So be it. I plan on re-reading my contribution when this booklet is published. And, hopefully, I won't offend myself. It's a slice of life from many years ago, and like some of Lovecraft's writings, should be taken in perspective … those who know me will recognize that back then, and to this day, I try to keep my tongue firmly planted in cheek.

Pissin' in the Wind
Or
Which Way to Baltimore, Jack?
Or
In Search of the Sixth World Fantasy Convention
(Four Cats Bop Their Way to Baltimore)

Scene: Providence, Rhode Island, Amtrak Passenger Station.

Time: 29 October 1980, somewhere around 11 p.m.

Characters: Jason Eckhardt, S. T. Joshi, Ryder Wyndham, Ken Neily, 'n me. Nearby are standing a crowd of other poor souls also about to get on a train headed towards New York, and then continuing on to Baltimore. These people keep clustered in a small group, have looks of disgust on their face, and attempt to keep away from the five main characters. Such is life. Especially when you have a group of Lovecraftians in a train station.

Ken (in a New Hampshire accent): Well, you know, you guys, I really wish that I could come along with you. I'd been looking forward to this convention for a long time . . . it's just one gawddam thing after another.

Others (in unison, amidst occasional belches): It surely won't be the same without you, Ken, but we'll be sure to pick up anything Lovecraftian that's obscure enough to go into your collection. Are you sure you don't want to jump on the train with us? . . .

Ken: I sure wish I could, guys, but you know how these gawddam things are . . . enjoy the trip and we'll see you Monday. (*Exit Ken.*)

On this sad note we boarded the train, heavy luggage in hand, arms, and where-ever. It was certainly a shame that Ken couldn't come along with us, but in his honour all we could do was try to have the best possible time without him. As it turned out we did have a good tine, a fact which I'm sure would have been amplified only with his presence. *Hélas.* New places and people to see, we were off on the Amtrak "Night Owl," and expected to arrive there the next morning somewhere around 7:30. It was to be a long night.

Porter (a black dressed in the usual garb, rolls his eyes and shouts over and over): Ahl abord, yessum, trainz 'bout to d'part. (*And then to himself:*) Lawdy, thos' white boys sur' ahr ah strang' lot.

Taking four seats which went across one aisle, there were S. T. and Ryder on one side of the train, with Jason and myself on the other side. Our best bet was to try to get some sleep on the train ride, as we probably wouldn't have a chance to sleep until the next night after we arrived at the hotel. It seems that I was the only one who was able to sleep rather constantly, the others claiming that the ride was too bumpy and noisy. I slept fine, at least until we went through the train station in the Big Apple. It was rather amusing as well as depressing to make this stop in the city which I loved so much. The people boarding the train there were typical New Yorkers, and I loved every moment of it: black couples going to visit relatives in Baltimore and Washington; Jewish businessmen going to Washington, most likely for an insurance conference. To me this was New York: blacks and Jews. It saddened me to think that I wouldn't be able to get off the train on this trip so that I might roam the city (there is little more exciting to me than visiting NYC). But all was not lost, for as I mentioned above, a good sampling of New York's population had boarded the train.

Trying to fall back asleep, I was detained by the voices of two black dudes, who sitting quite far to the rear of our car (appropriately enough, I chuckled) spoke in rather loud voices. "Sheeet, Otis, didja evah seee dat moveee 'Texas Chainsah Massacah'?" "Dat wuz one baaad moveee." "Yeah, 'n how 'bout . . ." They continued on like this for quite a while, discussing various gore flicks. If they had only known that there was a group of Lovecraftians in their car, a group which knew of even worst horrors, and a group—if they had been sitting closer to us—which could have shown them even worse horrors had they listened in on some of our conversations and escapades during that train ride . . .

Overall, the train ride was uneventful. I slept most of the time, thanks to these tiny pillows which Amtrak graciously supplied us with (resembling giant marshmallows), making me miss most of the boredom of an eight-hour train ride as well as the beautiful scenery throughout New Jersey (particularly Newark), Delaware, and Pennsylvania. What I do remember when waking up briefly somewhere between New Jersey and Delaware was seeing one of the most hideous sights which I've witnessed in my long twenty-one years on this planet. It didn't really make any difference what colour she was (she was black, and I imagine that she would have been ten times more hideous if she had been white, green, or any other colour, as a matter of fact). With lips that must have stuck out some two inches or so, she was quite horrible enough from the side from where I was

seeing her, but to add insult to injury (or some other silly analogy), her front teeth were pointing straight out of her mouth. I couldn't believe it at first and asked Jason and the others for their opinions on the matter. I was right! Our first encounter with a human can opener. With a smile on my face I fell back asleep, not to awake until we arrived in Baltimore.

Scene: Baltimore, Maryland, Ambrak Passenger Station.
Time: 30 October 1980, about 7:30 a.m.
Characters: Jason, S. T. Ryder, myself, as well as hundreds of train passengers who are cheering as we get off the train.

Marc: So, this is Baltimore.

Before me was one of the most disgusting cities which I've ever seen. It reeked of filth, poverty, and, over all, bad times.

S. T.: Well, you must remember that train stations are ordinarily in the worst part of town. We must check our luggage somewhere and then walk around; it is sure to get better.

S. T. was soon to eat his words, for as we found out, there are no better parts of Baltimore; in fact, they seem to get worse. Half the city appears to be burned down, the other half awaiting to be torched. We walked, and walked, and walked, for hours and hours, never finding anything which somewhat resembled civilisation. We did stop by some of the Poe sights, though they are few and far between.

The Poe House was of particular interest, though we never got to view its inside until after the convention started, the following Saturday evening. What was most striking about it was the fact that it was a recently renovated little cottage, quite charming, which sat in the middle of Baltimore's worst neighbourhood. Still, it was nice to see. We also walked past several other abodes inhabited by Poe at some time or another, as well as visiting the Enoch Pratt Library, famous for its fine Poe collection. While we didn't get a chance to witness their Poe memorabilia, they did have an excellent exhibit on H. L. Mencken, which was rather nice. Mencken was Baltimore's other famed citizen, and we all wondered why they didn't regard Lovecraft as highly in Providence as they did Poe here. Lovecraft was Providence's only famed author, aside from Les Daniels that is (Les is still living, therefore being unrecognised, but HPL has been dead for forty and some odd years, so there's really no excuse, now is there?).

From there we made our way to the Baltimore museum of art, which fortunately was somewhat outside of downtown Baltimore, and therefore in a slightly better neighbourhood (typical middle-class suburbia, with pretty flowers and ugly lawn statues). Here we came across several nice pieces, paintings by the likes of Matisse, Renoir, Monet, and a distant relative of mine, Delacroix. They also had one of Rodin's "The Thinking Man," though in this day and age, he took on more the look of the disgusted man, or better yet, the look of an EOD member waiting for the latest mailing. And then it was back to the train station (ugh!) to pick up our luggage, and then to begin our journey to the Marriott Hunt-Valley Inn.

Scene: Baltimore, Maryland, some main street in between downtown Baltimore and hunt Valley, at a bus stop.

Time: Midafternoon, I think.

Characters: A tired and disgruntled Jason, Ryder, S. T. and me.

Marc: I told you we should have taken a cab.

Others: The bus should be here any time.

One half hour later, the bus did arrive, but considering that to get to this bus stop, we had to take two other buses in a time span of two hours, it would have been cheaper for us to chip in $3–4 each and take a cab. Of course, even cheaper than a cab were the people I was with on this trip, and while I didn't mind waiting that long ordinarily, it's a slightly different story when you're in a place which is new and disgusting to you.

We finally did make it to the hotel, but were quite worn from the various bus rides. When we did make it there, no problems confronted us getting our room. As soon as we did get settled down, I immediately jumped into the shower—hadn't taken one since the previous day, and the train ride had left me feeling rather grimy.

Nothing momentous was to happen for a couple of hours, so I thought I might comment on the hotel. It is a very nice hotel, or better yet, more of a lodge. Its main point with me was that it's only three stories high, making visiting people from one room to another easy (how I hate waiting for elevators to the twentieth floor in big hotels). The one unfortunate part of the hotel is that if you have the slightest interests in eating, you have to eat in the hotel. There are no nearby restaurants, and to get to even the closest ones, you must have a car. Fortunately, we were prepared for this, and brought with us a good supply of food.

After running around a bit, and running into a few people, we were relaxing when Crispin came in. He—the poor soul—was to share the hotel room with us for the weekend, and we almost had the same gang reassembled which we had at Noreascon, Ryder—who, incidentally, is a friend of Jason's and ours from Little Compton, RI—taking the place of Ken Neily and Don Burleson, who, unfortunately, could not make the convention either.

Time began to fly by then and most of what happened is a blur and while I'm not sure I'm giving the convention enough credit, the entire weekend was somewhat uneventful, except for the brief instances which I'm about to mention. I've gone on too long as it is, so here goes . . .

Thursday night: Kirby McCauley had a party which we were all invited to. A small gathering, it had the one major characteristic found at all of Kirby's gatherings: plenty of booze. This party gave me a chance to see Bob Bloch again, for I hadn't

23

seen him in five years, not since the first Fantasycon. Sitting next to him was Fritz Leiber, and the three of us chatted for some time, particularly about the new book which I had just published on the first Fantasycon by Bloch, Leiber, and T. E. D. Klein (I was to see Ted later during the weekend). They were both quite pleased with it, and I was even more pleased that they were pleased. Unlike most publishers—especially those in the fantasy field—I *do* give a damn whether an author likes the way I treated his work or not; if not, I try to correct the problem. But they were both—as I already said—very pleased with the volume, and with this exchange, I knew the weekend was off to a good start. This party also marked my seeing Mollie Werba again, one whom I hadn't seen since the previous Christmas. As always, it was great seeing her.

Friday morning: This was a disaster. Artists were told to meet this person Joe Mayhew by the artroom at 8:30 that morning. Jason, who brought a great deal of work, went down to meet him, and I tagged along, just to see how things were running. Mayhew didn't arrive until 10 that morning, making everyone wait for him an hour and one half. When he did arrive, he did so brandishing a large sarcastic laugh as if to say "Look at these suckers waiting for me—I can mould them like putty in my hands." Along with his laugh, Mayhew also carried some 300 or so pounds of bulk weight, which leads me to say that he must be one of the biggest bastards I have ever encountered. Waiting with us were also Ryder (who also exhibited work at the con), Bob Lavoie, another RI artist, as well as Duncan Eagleson, from my home town of West Warwick. Duncan did the cover for the abovementioned volume I did on the first Fantasycon, and I will say here that it's one hell of a cover. The art show did finally get under way late that day, with no thanks to Mayhew, who had all the artists set up the entire show themselves.

Things picked up after this, I must say.

Friday evening: This was a very good night, for I had the honour of presenting to the convention John Strysik's film version of "The Music of Erich Zarin." This film, as you have probably all read by now, is, in my opinion, the best film adaptation of HPL done yet, and was received quite well by an appreciative audience. I chanced to speak to Fritz Leiber afterwards, along with Donald Sidney-Fryer, and they both loved the film. Fritz especially enjoyed the film, saying that he never thought that HPL could be so well captured on film. Donald was also impressed with it, agreeing with Fritz. I realise here that I have said little of Donald Sidney-Fryer. Never have I met such a charming gentleman as him; we met just a few days before the convention, as he was visiting with Don Grant, and I grew to like him immediately. I hope that the feeling is mutual.

Saturday was more of the same, seeing new people, etc. I had the pleasure of seeing Mark Sprague and his wife again, and both were fine. I also spent time speaking with Chet Williamson, talking about fantasy, and life in general—we hadn't seen each other since the second Fantasycon. Bernadette Bosky and I spoke about the ups and downs of going to college; her attitude was that I should continue on to graduate school next year, to meet new people as well as enjoying the sex and drugs which she said were "great in college"—my attitude was to get the hell out of academics, away from the pretensions of an artificial lifestyle (to each his/her own). I also spoke with Ben Indick, having not seen him since Fantasycon 2 as well.

Also a pleasure was meeting Bill Trotter, George Wetzel, and a lot of other people. I apologise if I've forgotten to mention you and you're reading this. Good seeing again were Dirk Mosig as well as Joe Smith, both of whom I had met for the first time at Fantasycon 5.

As I've already mentioned, I saw Ted Klein—though was sorely disappointed that he didn't get a Howard for his "Petey" but on the other hand was glad that it at least went to Ramsey Campbell and Elizabeth Lynn. While I haven't read any of Lynn's works, I imagine that Ted can't feel too bad about losing to someone as good as Ramsey.

And then it was especially good to see some other faithful from Providence: Bob Booth, Les Daniels, Bob Plante, as well as Don Grant. I was pleased to see Don get another Howard this year. Another winner of the Howard—and my number one choice for it this year—was Paul Allen, and I'm very happy for him; if anyone deserves it, he does.

And while on the subject of the Howard, the awards banquet was rather nice: at our table sat Mollie Werba, Vernon Shea, Bill Trotter, Allan Malancowicz, Jason Eckhardt, Ryder Windham, and Duncan and Susie Eagleson. Bob Bloch made a wonderful toastmaster, being at his wittiest best. Of course I had the advantage in appreciating some of his lines, such as "agents usually have their hands in authors' pockets, with the publishers keeping their hands in their own pockets." Of course, Bob said it better than that, but I think you get the idea. There was also another story which I swear only about one-fourth of the audience understood, but which had me in tears: "It's interesting that both Poe and H. L. Mencken came from the same city. Poe was the reserved author, gentlemanly and kind, while Mencken was a bawdy, invective critic. I enjoy both writers work very much. So when I arrived in Baltimore several days ago, the first thing I did was to go to Poe's grave and lay a wreath, and on Mencken's grave a volunteer."

Bob Bloch further amused us that Sunday night by spending some time with us in our hotel room. Gathered there were Mollie, Vernon, Ryder, Jason, Crispin, S. T., and myself. If Bob would have arrived just fifteen minutes earlier, he would have witness Jason, Mollie and S. T. trying to perform headstands on the floor while Vernon was dancing "jungle-style" in the corner. Things settled down, and Bob, myself, and the others spent much time punning over matters.

We left Monday morning and surprisingly enough, had no problems getting back to Providence. Ah, Providence! It was so good to be back, and while the convention had been enjoyable, Providence is, and will always be, my home, whether I live here or not later on in life. One week later, I recovered and while I don't expect to go to the California Fantasycon, I can always hope.

JASON ECKHARDT

The Bastard Sons of H. P. Lovecraft

In the Autumn of 1977 I was a freshman at the Rhode island School of Design in Providence. As many students did (and may yet do, for all I know), I used to grab the school's newspaper, the RISD Press, and peruse the latest attempts of student-cartoonists and shots of Providence cornices and corners by Photo Majors. This particular issue, however, escaped my attention until a friend pointed it out to me. In the "Classified" section was a small ad looking for illustrators of fantasy and horror. My friend (whose name, bless him, is lost to time), knowing my interest in such fiction, showed me the ad. I was only mildly interested until I read the last line of it—"Call Marc at Necronomicon Press." Anyone versed in the fiction of H. P. Lovecraft will recognize that Greek mouthful as one of Lovecraft's inventions. Lovecraft devotees in these days, when even a computer spell-checker recognises "Cthulhu" as a valid word, may find it hard to believe; but in 1977, "Necronomicon" was like the code-word to a secret society. I had been reading

Lovecraft since 1971, and had even attended the First World Fantasy Convention in Providence in '75. But aside from those giants at the convention—unapproachable demi-gods with names like Wellman, Campbell, Bloch and Long—I had met no one as interested in Lovecraft as myself.

Now, after a short phone call, I was face to face with such a creature. Marc Michaud was then a freshman at Brown University ("Up the Hill from RISD," he used to tease me); like me, eighteen, quiet and enthusiastic. We talked long that first evening in my dorm room at RISD, the upshot of which being he would send me word on the book he wanted me to illustrate. That turned out to be both the beginning of a long and fruitful work relationship, and of one of the most treasured friendships of my life. Through Marc I met S. T. Joshi, also a Brown student at the time; Ken Neily; Don Burleson; Sam Gafford; Ron and Herb Marshall; Mollie Werba (later Burleson); Peter Cannon; and many others. My world expanded geometrically that day in 1977.

Marc, S. T. and I found frequent reasons to get together in or near our rooms on College Hill. Even after I left RISD in December '78, I returned to Providence from my home in Little Compton, RI, as often as I could to attend meetings of "the gang"—or the Providence Pals, as we came to be semi-officially known. Like Lovecraft after his self-imposed seclusion, we began to travel. Ken proved invaluable in this regard. At a time when Marc, S. T. and I could not count a working car between us, Ken would show up in his battered station-wagon to squire us to any point we required. One trip from those early days that stands out to me was on the Yuletide of 1979. Marc, S. T. and I clambered aboard Ken's station-wagon and rode from Providence to Marblehead , Mass., in the deepening dusk of a cold, December day. It was the first time I laid eyes upon Marblehead, Lovecraft's "snowy Kingsport," and I was enthralled. It was also the first time I met Don Burleson, and his friend Tom Fletcher, who impressed us all by "skiing" down a set of ice-sheathed steps on his shoes. Don and Tom greeted us with a bellow of "YOG-SOTHOTH!!", a call that has become a tradition at Yuletide gatherings ever since. We walked the town, saw the sites in stark, haunting reality that I had only known before through fiction; watched the Yule-tide itself roll ominously up the shingle; and four days before my twenty-first birthday, I felt that I had been initiated into a very special group indeed. I was not wrong.

The beauty of the Providence Pals lay in the variety of experience and expertise that we brought to a shared interest. S. T. had his Classical background, Marc his editorial acumen; I brought an artist's eye to discussions of Lovecraft's work, and Ken a fresh and undiluted enthusiasm for the stories. Sam, my fellow artist, was also our resident William Hope Hodgson expert; Don added novel critical processes and a scathing humour to discussions; and so on. And every one of us could finish the couplet beginning, "That is not dead which can eternal lie…"

Several years ago there was a country music band called the Bastard Sons of Johnny Cash. I like to think of our crazy-quilt of a gang as the Bastard Sons (and Daughters, dear Mollie, Susan and Maddy) of H. P. Lovecraft; not children of his loins, but united by his vision and imagination; a shared vision that has brought me some of the best people of my life.

BEHIND THE MOUNTAINS OF MADNESS:
Lovecraft and the Antarctic in 1930
By Jason C. Eckhardt.

The short novel *At the Mountains of Madness* is one of the most powerful works in the oeuvre of H.P. Lovecraft and a recognised classic of horror literature. In many ways it is typical of Lovecraft's major works—the learned narrator, the pre-human civilization, and the "double-punch" climax—yet in other ways it is unique. But for the very beginning, the entire tale takes place in Antarctica, far away and far different from Lovecraft's usual New England settings. There is also extensive use of aircraft, and a very specific brand of aircraft, too. Why the differences?

It has been suggested that the setting is owed to Edgar Allan Poe's *The Narrative of A. Gordon Pym of Nantucket;* but while

Lovecraft is known to have been a great admirer of Poe and even makes references to Poe's story in his own (e.g., "*Tekili-li!*"), the two tales are very different. Limited by the nascent exploration of the region in his time, Poe's novel leaps into pure fantasy; whilst Lovecraft's, inspired and bolstered by twentieth century discoveries, leans into the just-forming genre of science fiction. So while Poe may have originally suggested the setting to Lovecraft, the younger writer used it in ways Poe would never have dreamed of.

Consider, rather, Lovecraft's own words on the frozen continent: "I think the Antarctic continent is really paramount in my geographic-fantastic imagination" (SL III.218). And this was not a new fascination, either: "About 1900 I became a passionate devotee of geography and history, and an intense fanatic on the subject of Antarctic exploration" (SL I.37). Then there is Lovecraft's extreme aversion to cold to consider. Antarctica, with temperatures often below -30°, would certainly hold much personal terror for a man who could not safely go out "at all under +20°, since the effects are varied and disastrous" (SL IV.83).

But there is also the basic consideration of size. In early 1931, when Lovecraft wrote the tale, where else could he have hidden two entire mountain ranges and the fantastically huge city of the Old Ones? Even the city of the Great Race of the later story "The Shadow out of Time" had to be buried in order for it to be discovered. No, *At the Mountains of Madness* demanded a colossal stage and undiscovered marvels to encompass both its physical requirements and epic content.

And what of the "large Dornier aëroplanes"?[1] Their presence in the story is central, for it is in them that Lake and his expedition (and later Dyer and his crew) reach the Mountains of Madness and what lay beyond them. It can be argued that the airplane is much faster than dog-team or tractor for exploring; but in a work of fiction, where periods of weeks or months can be condensed into a sentence or two, this hardly matters. To understand the use of airplanes (and Dornier airplanes specifically) and setting in this story, a brief examination of South Polar exploration of the period is called for.

Prior to Lovecraft's birth (1890) there had been various voyages of importance around Antarctica, particularly those of Cook, Ross, and Wilkes. But it was not until after the turn of the twentieth century and the emergence of a new class of explorer that the "Heroic Age" of exploring began. Roald Amundsen first attainted the South Pole in 1911, followed only a month later by the ill-fated Capt. Robert F. Scott. There were important expeditions by Carstens E. Borchgrevink (whose adventure was followed closely by the then ten year old Lovecraft; cf. SL I.37); Sir Ernest Shackleton in 1904, 1914, and 1922; Dr. Charcot (1903-05); Sir Douglas Mawson (1911-14 and 1929-31); and others all through the teens and twenties.[2] Human flight came to Antarctica on February 4, 1902, when Capt. Scott rose 800

---

[1] Lovecraft, At the Mountains of Madness and Other Novels (Sauk City, WI: Arkham House, 1985), p.4. Hereafter cited in the text as MM.

[2] William H. Kearns, Jr., and Beverly Britton, The Silent Continent (New York: Harper & Brothers, 1955), pp.227-30.

feet from the ice in a balloon,[3] but powered flight would be more than twenty years later in coming.

Yet for all this furious activity, the Antarctic remained stubbornly inviolable. The coldest, windiest, highest and driest continent awaited the development of safer and more efficient means of human travel; and, in its extreme cold, regularly swallowed up the lives of even the most seasoned of explorers.

This brings us to the period 1928-31 and another reason for the setting of *At the Mountains of Madness*. During this time four major expeditions laid siege to the ice and snow: the Wilkins-Hearst Expedition (1928-29); the Riiser-Larsen Expedition (1929-30); the Australasian Expedition of 1929-31; and the first Byrd Expedition (1928-30). All four bear an important similarity to Lovecraft's fictional Miskatonic Expedition—the use of aircraft. One of them bears a suspiciously large number of similarities to Lovecraft's.

---

[3] W.L.G. Joerg, <u>A Brief History of Polar Exploration Since the Introduction of Flying</u> (New York: American Geographic Society, 1930), p. 3.

The Wilkins-Hearst Expedition, led by famed aeronaut Sir Hubert Wilkins, landed on Deception Island (cf. map) in November 1928. From this base Wilkins became the first in powered flight over Antarctica on December 30, 1928. Other flights "proved" that the Palmer Peninsula was an archipelago. The Riiser-Larsen Expedition was headed by Hjalmar Riiser-Larsen, one-time pilot for Amundsen. He explored by ship and two airplanes the coast from Enderby Land to Seal Bay on the Weddell Sea, discovering several previously unknown land and submarine areas. Mawson's 1929-31 expedition (really two expeditions—1929-30 and 1930-31) sailed much of the long coast of Wilkes Land and part of Enderby Land, and, like Riiser-Larsen, made extensive use of the aircraft they brought.[4] (Lovecraft's narrator in *At the Mountains of Madness* (MM 103) voices concern that Mawson and his men might explore too near the greater mountain range of the story; but though they were in that general area at the time, Mawson's expedition was spared any such monstrous revelations.)

That Lovecraft knew of these expeditions is likely; but that he knew of the Byrd Expedition cannot be doubted. It would be far more difficult to believe that he didn't know about it, and a lot about it, too. Led by Rear Admiral Richard E. Byrd, hero of the first North Polar flight as well as many others, the expedition was covered by most major newspapers, the August 1930 issue of *National Geographic*, and in Byrd's own book, *Little America* (first published in October 1930, it was already in its third printing by the end of the year).[5] Lovecraft wrote *At the Mountains of Madness* between February and March 22, 1931,[6] so would have had plenty of time to read any of these sources and adapt the information to his own use. The idea of a story about a lost Arctic or Antarctic civilization had been with him for

---

[4] Kearns and Britton, pp. 230-31.

[5] Richard E. Byrd, Jr., Little America (New York: G.P. Putnam's Sons, 1930), copyright page.

[6] Kenneth W. Faig, Jr., H. P. Lovecraft: His Life, His Work (West Warwick, RI: Necronomicon Press, 1979), p. 35.

years at this point,[7] but it is clear that all the exploring activity must have provided him with fresh inspiration and a framework based in fact. Here follows an examination of just how closely the two expeditions, Byrd and Miskatonic, resemble each other.

The Byrd Expedition, with 42 members (excluding ships' crews), about 100 dogs, a Ford snow-tractor, wireless equipment, geological equipment, and three airplanes, departed New York Harbor on August 25, 1928.[8] The Miskatonic Expedition leaves Boston Harbor almost exactly two years later, on September 2, 1930, bringing with it a land expedition of 20 men, 55 dogs, wireless and geological research equipment, and five airplanes (MM 6f). Both expeditions travel in two ships (Byrd's in the *City of New York* and the *Eleanor Bolling*; Lovecraft's in the brig *Arkham* and the barque *Miskatonic*), and both pass westward through the Panama Canal. Byrd stopped at Dunedin, New Zealand, for supplies; while the two Miskatonic ships dock at Hobart, Tasmania, for final supplies. After the ice-pack forced one of Byrd's ships to turn back, the other finally reached the Bay of Whales on December 28, 1928; and it was here that was erected their famous base, "Little America". Across the great Ross Ice Shelf at Ross Island, Loveraft's protagonists land at the foot of Mt. Erebus on November 9, 1930, and unload their "drilling apparatus, dogs, sledges, tents, provisions, gasoline tanks, experimental ice-melting outfit, cameras both ordinary and aërial, aëroplane parts and other accessories." (MM 8). Both parties lift their aircraft from the ships directly onto the ice-barrier for assembly; but unlike Byrd, Lovecraft preferred to keep his main base of operations aboard his ships. (Byrd sent his ships north on February 21, 1929, to keep them from becoming locked in the ice. Lovecraft's expedition didn't stay into the Antarctic winter, so this wasn't a problem for them.)

---

[7] "Lost Arctic and Antarctic civilisations form a fascinating idea to me—I used it once in 'Polaris' and expect to use it again..." (SL III.38). "Polaris" was written in 1918.

[8] Edwin P. Hoyt, The Lost Explorer: The Adventures of Admiral Byrd (New York: John Day Co., 1968), pp. 165-250.

A word here about the Antarctic cold. Along about this point, Lovecraft's narrator Dyer says that "our experience with New England winters" (MM 9) had prepared them for the 0° to +25° temperatures they encounter on the ice. This echoes the fact that several of Byrd's men trained in Labrador and New Hampshire preparatory to the South Polar trip. This also points up Lovecraft's idea of really cold temperatures, temperatures which would be considered balmy at the South Pole itself.

At this point in both expeditions, the aircraft come into play. Byrd made a flight on January 26, 1929, heading eastward into Edward VII Land and discovering the Rockefeller Mountains. Lovecraft's Dyer and his companions fly almost due south on November 21, 1930, cross Beardmore Glacier and establish a second base at Latitude 86° 7' South, Longitude 174° 23' East. (This is one part of the narrative, airplanes aside, which owes more to the journeys of Scott and Shackleton than to that of Byrd. Both Scott and Shackleton journeyed south toward the Pole over Beardmore Glacier from bases on Ross Island. Lovecraft's characters also recreate Shackleton's ascent of Mt. Erebus in 1908.[9])

The Miskatonic's southern base is reminiscent of the string of supply bases set up by Byrd in October 1929, after the long inaction of the Antarctic winter. Such bases were essential because of the restricted range of aircraft at that time. From this southern base Lovecraft sends a party of three to scale Mt. Fritjof Nansen on December 13-15, and a flight of two of the Dornier airplanes over the South Pole on January 6, 1931. This recalls the groundbreaking flight Byrd and three others took over the South Pole on November 28-29, 1929, using the big Ford Tri-motor airplane, the "Floyd Bennett". Details of this flight bring up what may be more than an interesting coincidence. On Byrd's flight southward, the plane was required to cross a high pass between two mountains, one of which was the Mt. Nansen Lovecraft's men would scale. There were 15,000 pounds of fuel, provisions and equipment aboard the "Floyd Bennett", including several hundred pounds of photographic equipment; and it was only by dumping out 250

---

[9] Kearns and Britton, p. 228.

lbs. of *food* (considered, incredibly, the least important item aboard) that the fliers were able to clear the ice and bleak rocks of the pass. This is highly reminiscent of Dyer and Danforth's flight over the pass in the Mountains of Madness, in a "lightened plane with aërial camera and geologist's outfit" (MM 40).

The Miskatonic's biologist Lake makes a preliminary sledging and boring journey on January 11-18, 1931; and on the 22nd, with eleven men, 36 dogs and four of the five Dornier aircraft, he flies over 700 miles northwestward. At Latitude 76° 15' South, Longitude 113° 10' East, Lake radios that they have spotted an enormous mountain chain.[10] After some observation flights over the foothills and the exhumation of the Old Ones, Lake's group prepares to weather a storm that rushes upon them from the heights. (Interestingly, the area in Wilkes Land where Lovecraft places the end of his mountains *is* close to the windiest place on earth. Winds of 200 miles an hour have been reported there.[11]) Here again we must look back at a remarkable similarity between Lovecraft's and Byrd's expeditions. On March 7, 1929, three members of Byrd's party flew to the base of the newly discovered Rockefeller Mountains for geological research. They were forced to remain there by the onset of a storm, and attempted to secure their plane from wind damage by tying it to stakes in the ground and erecting a small snow-block wall around it. Despite these precautions, the gale's end found the plane torn apart by the wind's fury. The explorers were rescued two weeks later by Byrd himself. Similarly, when Dyer arrives with a rescue party on January 25, they find Lake's camp in the following condition:

---

[10] These coordinates should be taken as the *airplane's* location at the time of the sighting and not that of the mountains. Using the description of the mountain range of p. 70 of the Arkham House edition, these coordinates would still put Lake 100 miles away from the range. This is possible, given the immensity of the chain and the altitude of the aircraft; and likely, too, since they fly for another half hour (75 miles, at their probable rate of speed) before being forced down in the foothills. See map for reference.

[11] James M. Darley, National Geographic Society Map of Antarctica, February 1963.

It is a fact that the wind wrought dreadful havoc . . . One aëroplane shelter—all, it seems, had been left in a far too flimsy and inadequate state—was nearly pulverised; and the derrick at the distant boring was entirely shaken to pieces. The exposed metal of the grounded planes and drilling machinery was bruised to a high polish, and two of the tents were flattened despite their snow banking. (MM31-32)

Dyer and Danforth cross the great mountain chain on January 26, explore the city beyond, and return the same day. The rescue expedition, in three of the planes, returns to the southern base on the 27th, thence back to Ross Island on the 28th. The ships *Arkham* and *Miskatonic*, with all the surviving members of the expedition aboard, pull away from the ice shelf on February 2, 1931. Byrd's expedition, after another exploratory flight over the Ross Ice Shelf, quit the Antarctic on February 18, 1930.

Thus we have the two expeditions, fact and fiction. Some similarities were certainly dictated by mere practicality; it was standard operating procedure, for example, to plan operations in the Antarctic between September and February, the Southern Spring and Summer, when conditions were not so severe. Yet it is clear that Lovecraft, though not intending to "cash in" on the popularity of Byrd's exploits, certainly admired the man and his achievements enough to use them as a basis for his own flights of fancy.

As for differences between the two, one of the major ones is the direction of exploration (Byrd to the east, Lovecraft to the northwest). But even here Lovecraft explains that his group originally intended to head "500 miles to the eastward" (MM11) from the southern camp. That he sent them the other way is due to the far more unknown aspect of the northwest. As no one had yet explored it, there was no one to gainsay his creations there. Another difference is in time spent---Byrd was there fifteen months to Miskatonic's three. This discrepancy is due to two factors. One is the disaster at Lake's camp; they might have stayed another year but for the horrific circumstances. Two is extremely good luck on the part of Lovecraft's people. Even the narrator of Lovecraft's tale says, "Our good luck and efficiency were almost uncanny" (MM 11). Compare, for example, the Miskatonic expedition to Byrd's second expedition of 1933-35, during which the camp doctor became seriously ill, four of their five snow-tractors either broke down or burned, and Byrd himself almost suffocated while alone and far from help.[12] Notwithstanding the horrors in the Old Ones' city, the Miskatonic crew was lucky indeed!

Given the state of exploration, then, it's easy to see why the airplanes appear in the story. But why Dornier airplanes and not Trimotors like Byrd's? To answer this, we must look to the adventures of that other great polar hero, Roald Amundsen. In 1924 Amundsen and American adventurer Lincoln Ellsworth prepared to fly over the North Pole. The airplane upon which they finally decided for the flight was the Dornier Do-J "Wal", a two-engine, single-wing flying boat used primarily for passenger service. In his book *Beyond Horizons* Ellsworth explains the pilot's choice:

> In the first place, he sought a ship with a duralumin hull. Wooden hulls he deemed unsuitable for landing on rough ice or in water filled with broken ice, because of the danger of stripping the bottom. Duralumin, even lighter than steel, will bend or dent under ordinary collisions but will not break much more readily than wood.
>
> Several types of duralumin flying boats were then made in Europe. What determined the choice of the Dornier-Wal [sic] was the design of the hull itself. The lines of other hulls were such that in snow they would push the snow aside, in the manner of a plow. The Dornier-Wal had a lift forward that would enable it to climb over snow,

---

[12] Hoyt, pp. 280-333.

like a toboggan, and was the only hull of that design in Europe.[13]

On the Antarctic continent concern for drift ice would be unfounded; but the duralumin, an alloy of aluminum, would still be protection against sastrugi, the odd ice-ripples found there. The handling in show is more apt, since most of the Antarctic is, of course, snow.

Ellsworth goes on to explain the advantages of the two Rolls-Royce engines, one of which could keep the plane in the air and both of which could lift the plane plus its own weight in cargo (about 8,000 lbs.). Further, these engines contained heaters to keep oil and water from freezing, and 4% glycerine was added to the water to keep it liquid down to -17° Celsius.[14]

These were modifications peculiar to the two Dorniers that Amundsen used. Of the 300 or so of the planes built, there were more than twenty versions and many individual modifications.[15] This fits in well with Lovecraft's narrator's statement about their "huge planes built to our especial orders for heavy machinery transportation" (MM27), planes "designed especially for the tremendous altitude flying necessary on the antarctic plateau and with added fuel-warming and quick starting devices: (MM4). With a 73-foot wingspan, [16] the Wal would certainly qualify for the narrator's description as "huge".

As for the range of flight, the farthest the planes in the story are required to fly in one jump is 700 miles (from the southern camp to Lake's camp) and the Dornier Wal was capable of nearly twice that (1,368 miles).[17] Of course, they planned to get back, too; but that could have been accomplished by ferrying fuel in one of the planes, just as they did from Ross Island to the southern base (MM 12).

---

[13] Lincoln Ellsworth, Beyond Horizons (Garden City, NY: Doubleday, Doran, 1938), pp. 145-46.

[14] Hjalmar Riiser-Larsen, et al., Our Polar Fight: The Amundsen-Ellsworth Polar Flight (New York: Dodd, Mead, 1925), p. 153.

[15] John Stroud, European Transport Aircraft since 1910 (Fallbrook, CA: Aero Publishers, 1966), p. 239.

[16] Stroud, p. 242.

[17] Ibid.

Another important factor in the plane's appropriateness for this task would be its weight capacity. Using calculations worked up by Rear Admiral Byrd in *Little America*[18] and specifications for the Dornier Wal, the following possible check-list is submitted for Lake's sub-expedition for a sixty-day excursion:

ITEM(S)	WEIGHT
12 men	2,400 lbs.
36 dogs (80 lbs. each)	2,880
Human food	2,160
Dog food	3,888
3 Sledges (long Norwegian freight sledges)	153
Dog gear	36
Navigation, surveying and meteorological equipment	91
Radio gear	300
Safety devices	40
Tools	20
Personal equipment	700
Gasoline	9,000
TOTAL	21,688 lbs.

Considering that each Dornier Wal was capable of carrying 7,000 pounds of cargo, it's plain that Lake's four Dorniers could handle what this trip required of it, plus room for extra gasoline and Peabodie's drilling and melting apparatus (about which we can only guess the weight).

There are a couple of differences between the historical Wal and the planes mentioned in *At the Mountains of Madness*, though. One is the "landing skis" Lovecraft mentions (MM 49), and another is the narrator's comment about getting "*the engine* started (MM 104-my italics, JCE), implying one as opposed to the Wal's two engines. As for the skis, it's been shown that the Wals wouldn't need them; but on the other

---

[18] Byrd, pp. 257, 261, 277.

hand, they couldn't hurt. Most planes attempting the Antarctic, even today, sport skis. Regarding the engines, the Wal's two engines were housed in one nacelle, which could easily have been mistaken by Lovecraft for one engine. The main problem with the Dornier Wal for the Miskatonic Expedition's uses is its ceiling or maximum altitude. Lovecraft has his plane clearing a pass of 24,000 feet, more than twice the ceiling of the Wal. However, we must take Lovecraft's word that his planes were "designed especially for the tremendous altitude flying necessary", and allow him some artistic license.

Finally, a note on the mountains themselves. There are, unfortunately (or fortunately), no such "Mountains of Madness" in that part of Antarctica; but happily this was never disproved during Lovecraft's lifetime. "I have to stop dreaming about an unknown realm (such as Antarctica or Arabia Deserta) as soon as the explorers enter it" (SL III.140). So wrote Lovecraft in 1930, and we are all the more fortunate that the explorers stayed away just long enough for him to complete his story. The real "Mountains of Madness" (the highest in Antarctica, anyway) were discovered in 1935, only four years after Lovecraft composed his short novel, by Lincoln Ellsworth on the first trans-Antarctic flight. He and his pilot passed far to the west of them and christened them the Sentinel Mountains. But, as with the characters in At the Mountains of Madness, a haze hid the highest peaks from them. Ellsworth and his pilot considered them a minor range, unaware that the 14,000 peak of Vinson Massif lay just beyond their sight. Earlier on the flight, the airmen had found and named the Eternity Range, for reasons that sound remarkably like something Lovecraft might have said:

> We were indeed the first intruding mortals in
> this age-old region, and looking down on the
> mighty peaks I thought of eternity and man's
> insignificance.[19]

So stands Lovecraft's novel as a monument to his ability to weld reality and imagination into powerful art.

---

[19] Ellsworth, p.320.

DON BURLESON

For about seventeen years after first reading Lovecraft in 1955 at the age of 12, I pursued my interest in his work all alone, seldom in those days meeting anyone else who had even heard of him. But all that was to change.

If any one person was responsible for getting me into the company of other admirers of Lovecraft, it was Frank Belknap Long, with whom I went out of my way to start a regular correspondence, and whom I was to meet face to face at the First World Fantasy Con in 1975 in Providence. Frank put me in touch with Lovecraft scholar Dirk Mosig, who in turn (in the midst of an intense Lovecraft-style letter exchange) arranged for me to be on a panel discussion with him at the 1978 World Science Fiction Convention (Iguanacon) in Phoenix. S.T. Joshi, whom I had never met, was on that panel too, and back in New England he would soon enough introduce me to the rest of the gang.

I had of course already visited Providence a number of times before I knew anybody there (once even being shown into the fabled cellar of the Shunned House on Benefit Street), but now when I roamed about College Hill and Swan Point, it was in the company of such personages as S.T., Ken Neily, Jason Eckhardt, Ron Marshall, and Marc Michaud, as well as (later on) Bob Price, Sam Gafford, and others. Before meeting any of these folks, I had already started the now legendary Yulefest by visiting Marblehead every December 21st by myself or with my friend Tom Fletcher. Later, others were appearing there as well. This was many years before computers and social media, and it was amazing how the faithful had a way of just showing up even when nothing had been arranged! "Only the poor and the lonely remember."

But loneliness wasn't forever. After Mollie and I were together, I brought her to those hallowed Kingsport byways and, in company with the other Providence Pals, we would enjoy indulgences ranging from scholarly discussions to shouting "Yog-Sothoth!" from the graveyard on the hill, to playing catch with a frozen dog turd. Those were the days. Cthulhu fhtagn!

What Came Up over Dinner
By Donald Burleson

By some perverse inclination of an indifferent cosmos, a house and a parcel of land may so resemble, in general aspect, the resident family, as somewhat to prepare the uninformed visitor for beholding the nature of those denizens dwelling within. This tendency of the outward impression to mirror the beings that it shelters may be more than a mere proclivity of certain personalities to keep up their property in certain ways— it is, rather, as if the persons in question manage, by osmotic and probably unwitting gradations, to lend their most fundamental qualities to the place that gives them lodging.

And so it was with the Moore farm, a remote and dilapidated cluster of weed-choked structures in which the crumbling farmhouse itself scarcely stood out as looking any more habitable than the miserable and equally malodorous outbuildings. A general air of desolation hung over all. Woebegone willows drooped their unhealthy fronds over a ground so parched and untended that only a robust imagination could ever have connected it with farming and cultivation, and the buildings themselves looked as if the world, off in pursuit of more promising enterprises, had forgotten them utterly, leaving them to their bleak dissolution over the unsympathetic years. It was an unwholesome place.

In the kitchen of the farmhouse, on one gray and dismal afternoon with a grumble of melancholy thunder in the air, Ralph Moore and his slatternly wife Millicent sat at the table over a cheerless meal. Ralph was a grizzled old wreck of a farmer, toothless but for one yellowed upper fang in the middle of his mouth. He was a bleary-eyed and corpulent man of sixty-three who gave the impression of being much older. Poor Millicent had fared little better over the years, her thinning greasy hair a rodent-like gray having none of the gentle charm of advancing years, with only the brutal cares of an unpleasant life stamped upon her wrinkled saurian face. Ralph and Millicent were unappealing creatures, as both decorum and cleanliness had long since departed from their persons and their environs.

Millicent watched Ralph pushing sinewy chicken and wilted green beans and slices of mushy tomatoes and overcooked biscuits into his mouth. It spoiled her appetite for her own dinner. With clear disdain, she eyed the way his grotesquely prominent paunch bulged against the edge of the table. "Don't you ever stop eating?" she asked.

His rheumy eyes narrowed upon her as he replied almost incomprehensibly with a slavering mouthful of wetly churned food: "What does it matter to you?" He emitted a ghastly belch. "Besides, it ain't that I eat too much. This belly, I mean. Fact is, I haven't been going to the toilet a lot."

Even as accustomed as she was to his habit of giving voice to unsavory topics at the table, she wrinkled her face in disgust. "How long since you went?"

Ralph's bewhiskered cheeks ballooned again in a raucous belch. "Dunno. Been weeks."

His wife's eyes widened as much as they were capable of doing. "Weeks? Weeks? You mean to tell me you've been holding all that—"

He wheezed with laughter, letting a stream of yellow drool escape down his dirty shirt-front. "Maybe I like being full of—"

"You filthy old pig!" she yelled, and gave the rickety table a sharp push into his stomach.

The reaction was swift and spectacular. Ralph roared like some deranged beast, and a vile, multicolor cascade of vomit issued from his gaping mouth. Thick gobbets of it went onto his plate, into his coffee mug, over the tabletop, all over Millicent's face, indeed all over the room. The pale red of tomato slices, the dull green of the beans, the fleshy strands of chicken, the damp chunks of biscuit all hung steaming and dripping everywhere they landed.

And more was coming, because Ralph's roaring had been only a dim prelude. Now, the room reverberant with it, a rumbling like the eruption of some vast sea-bottom volcano came forth from his throat and ever-enlarging mouth, a tortured and bloody mouth that tore more widely open to let out an unthinkable torrent of what once might have been food. Greasy clots of undefinable matter spewed forth upon the noisome air, a nightmare of gray, quivering, wormy shapes that splattered and fragmented everywhere. One particularly loathsome strand of something quite long and limp that could have been unchewed and partially digested asparagus wrapped itself like a leech across Millicent's mouth, muffling her screams. As more and more came up, it took on the aspect more of a festering and rotten mess of fecal matter than of food, as if Ralph's purulent and necrotic insides had backed all the way up like a cesspool and ejected themselves out his mouth, an avalanche of clabbered sewage.

Millicent, weighted down by what had hit her, both physically and otherwise, spilled over backward in her chair, tumbling onto the floor. Blindly desperate, she began scrambling to get up, but the horror from Ralph's eruption was all over her, sentient, searching, finding.   Soon she was unmoving and silent.   Ralph was silent now too, in his chair, his heart still, his shattered mouth still redly agape, his jaundiced eyes bulging but seeing nothing.

One can only surmise that what came up over dinner took possession of the house and grounds—grew, proliferated, expanded, prevailed, insinuating itself first into every corner of the old house and then, finding its way out the windows, burrowing into the soil. Today if one ventures near the place, one sees a sort of spongy admixture to the fetid earth, a kind of froth that, examined more closely, might be found to undulate faintly, even when there is no wind to stir it, and might reasonably be supposed to contain a certain essence of the tragically ill-starred Ralph Moore. He was, after all, a man of the soil.

MOLLIE BURLESON

I first "met" Lovecraft around 1950, when I saw Orson Welles read "The Rats in the Walls" on TV. I was stunned. Later I searched for Lovecraft at libraries, book sales, and just about everywhere. Finally in 1971 I found a copy of *Best Supernatural Stories of H. P. Lovecraft*. I wrote an inscription in it stating how happy I was to find it! That led to my visiting Providence in 1978, and at first I couldn't find anyone who knew of HPL, even at Brown University. Then someone referred me to Brown University Bookstore, where I discovered Marc Michaud's many publications. I was hooked. I returned to Providence in 1979 for the Fifth World Fantasy Con, where I met Don, S.T., Vernon Shea, and many others.

But being one of the Providence Pals started for me when I moved to New Hampshire and married Don. He took me to Marblehead (Kingsport, as I soon learned), and we met Ken Neily there to celebrate the real Yuletide. What a wonderful experience that was. We went there for fifteen years, never missing a one. We went in sleet, snow, ice, rain, etc. In time, other lovers of HPL joined us: Marc Michaud, S.T. Joshi, Ron Marshall, Bob Price, Jason Eckhardt, and so many more. I gave the original members new names: Don was Opener of the Way, S.T. was Keeper of the Flame, Jason was Illustrator of the Tableau, Marc was Chronicler of the Word, Bob Price was Hierophant of the Horde, and I was Bard of the Convocation. On each 21st, Don would stand on the steps of the church, prototype of the one in "The Festival," and recite from it with all of us looking on, beginning with "The nethermost caverns are not for the fathoming of eyes that see." We then climbed up to the cemetery on the hill overlooking the harbor, and yelled, "Yog Sothoth!" and "Cthulhu lives!" Moments never to be forgotten. We miss the Gang, but remember them every 21st of December. Ia! Shub-Niggurath!

Out There

By Mollie Burleson

(Inspired by H. P. Lovecraft's poem "Nemesis")

The Universe turns,
Expands,
Grows.
The black planets roll unheeded
Nameless
Lustreless
Dumb.
They roll and tumble and boil—
And die.
And are born.
Black holes stretch and yawn and beckon;
Red giants cool.
White-hot stars bubble, explode, shooting out
Messages to deaf worlds.
Comets probe billion-starred voids
Past gibbering novas and fragmented moons.
Whirling bits of primal rock float forever
And fall unnoticed upon forgotten planets,
While hollow suns glare blindingly down
On pock-marked surfaces
Tortured by howling idiot winds.

Suns are born,
Suns die,
And still the cycle spins
Without aim or cognizance
Of what it does.
Like some gigantic insane creature
It blunders drunkenly along fury-haunted spaces
Alone.

BOB PRICE

The Statement of Robert M. Price

My involvement with the infamous Providence Pals began innocently enough back in 1980 with an innocuous visit to a Thayer Street bookstore when I stumbled upon a volume that told the way past hidden screens that keep lost aeons to their own demesnes. It was a copy of *Lovecraft Studies*. I had been a devotee of both Lovecraftian fiction and scholarly journals for some years already, but a scholarly journal *about Lovecraft*? Needless to say, I bought it. In no time flat I had submitted an article, "Higher Criticism and the *Necronomicon*," and thus made the glad acquaintance of the youthful, brilliant, and cocky editor S.T. Joshi. He graciously invited me to enter the circle of HPL enthusiasts who met two or three times a year in Providence, College Hill, where Lovecraft once lived and where Joshi now replaced him. I made my first *hajj* to the holy city in October, 1981, the same week I had just met the wonderful Carol Selby, she who would become my life-elevating wife. I sent her a postcard from Providence, and it wasn't long before she was able to accompany me to some of the meetings.

Back in those days, I was slim, had mainly black hair, and was easily able both to wolf down great pizza at Minerva's (still can) and to walk the quaint and charming streets for our ritual tours of houses where Lovecraft had lived, calling up to the windows, "Can Howard come out to play?" (okay, just kidding on that one), and sites mentioned, thinly veiled if veiled at all, in his stories. It never ceased to be a thrill. I can't drag my rotting, bloated carcass around so easily anymore, but I rejoice to see a younger generation of fans making the sacred circuit.

These were exciting times for the Providential Pals, as we discussed the progress of S.T.'s massive Lovecraft bibliography (threatening to eclipse Lovecraft's own writings in length!) and his ongoing task of textual criticism. Mastermind and magnate Marc Michaud would update us on his latest Necronomicon Press projects, and Jason Eckhardt would unveil his newest shocking works of Pickmanesque depravity. Don Burleson had not yet invited pariah status by embracing Deconstruction (neither had I, nor even heard of it!). Sam Gafford hadn't yet moved on to Machen and Hodgson.

I once remarked to Peter Cannon how delighted I was to have fallen in with such a group of dedicated, enterprising, and all-around noble people. Marc had recently penned an essay called "Why I Am not a 'Fan,'" which reminds me of the old saw, "I wouldn't want to be part of any club that would have someone like me as a member." But he was right: these people, though forming a true literary cult, had a professional, artistic, and scholarly seriousness that one does not necessarily expect to find among fandom. Come to think of it, that shouldn't have been surprising given the depth of the subject matter that so fascinated us (and still does). I mean, I have always loved *Star Wars* (at least the first two, 1977 and 1980), but if anyone were to publish *Star Wars Studies*, it would automatically be a parody. And those who did not realize that would be just the sort of "fans" from whom Marc hastened to differentiate himself (and us).

Occasionally I catch up with various of the aging Pals at a Lovecraftian convention, where we are, incredibly, esteemed as elder statesmen. It makes me recall those times with the Providence Pals back in the 80s, and even with the terrific things we have severally undergone and accomplished since then, I guess I still think of those times as the glory days. Boy, do I miss 'em.

The Fish Monger
By Robert M. Price

Somehow or other, Howard Phillips Lovecraft of Providence, Rhode Island, had never gotten around to eating fish—not that he remembered, anyway. No particular reason. His mother simply had never served it. Perhaps she did not like it. But dietary habits form early and do not easily change. Nonetheless, Lovecraft was about to make a discovery. He was home alone; his aunts were away for a week, visiting an ill cousin even more elderly than them. Howard did not mind; even though he loved the old ladies (right out of *Arsenic and Old Lace*), he thoroughly enjoyed his solitude. He could double his reading, fiction writing, and correspondence. But that did not make him immune to nuisances. Muttering curses under his breath, he got up to answer the door, or actually, to dispatch whomever it was who was so intent on interrupting his work. No aficionado of spectral fiction, that was for sure.

HPL took his sweet time getting to the door, but when he opened it, his caller was still there.

"Yes? What is it?" That was about as rude as Lovecraft, a gentleman, allowed himself to get.

The man standing there was quite tall and, though he was neatly dressed, his threadbare suit was too small for his stature. Of all things, he was holding out a fish for Lovecraft's inspection. So, a fish peddler. Lovecraft could see the man's refrigerated truck parked at the curb. He was curiously reminiscent of a mail carrier, as if he meant to deliver some message written in fins and scales.

"Good day, sir! I'm new to Providence. Just moved here from Essex County, Massachusetts. I figure there's nobody that don't like good fish, an' I got the best! Yes sir, I got sea food here like you'll find nowhere else!"

Lovecraft could not evaluate this claim, as he had only the remotest idea of the variety of fishes and their dapper looks. He pretended to listen to the uncouth man's sales pitch as long as he could stand it, then tried to cut in with the announcement that he had to get back to work. When this failed to stop the man, Lovecraft snapped, "All right, my man. How much?" He produced the desired coins and received the newspaper-wrapped fish corpse into reluctant hands, then kicked the fanlight door shut. He made straight for the kitchen and deposited his smelly burden in the ice box. His aunts could do what they pleased with the thing. Back to his desk and fountain pen. And some monsters.

*

The aunts returned on schedule, and Howard was happy to see them. He had no thought for the fish, but around suppertime, Aunt Lillian knocked gently on his door. "Howard?"

Of course, she had discovered the fish and wanted to know if her nephew wanted it baked or fried. Turning around in his swivel chair, Howard paused and pondered. He couldn't remember seeing the old ladies eating fish, though we probably couldn't have remembered anything they ate. It must be the same thing they served him, and he certainly had not consumed any seafood. But what if the aunts did not favor fish? It would not be fair for him to turn up his long nose while they felt they had to eat it so as not to let it go to waste.

"Baked, thanks."

When he sat down to eat, Howard was quite surprised, and a little amused at his own expense, to see that he was the only diner with fish looking back at him. The old women appeared slightly embarrassed. "Howard dear, we don't really care for fish. Besides, there's not really enough for all three of us. And since you bought it special, we thought we'd let you have the whole thing."

Lovecraft chuckled and stabbed his supper with a well-aimed fork. Chewing thoughtfully, he mused silently: "Not bad, really. A little strange tasting, but then I'm new to fish."

He sat down again at his desk and took up an unfinished letter to a West Coast correspondent, a Mister Joshi, an Indian on whom he had jokingly based his character Swami Chandraputra, just as he had made Clark Ashton Smith into the Atlantean hierophant Klarkash-ton. But he found that his always delicate stomach began to rumble. He hoped that his dinner was not about to rise up like R'lyeh from the deep. Maybe it was time to head for bed, though not, he hoped, for strange aeons.

Lovecraft was no stranger to bizarre dreams. In fact he welcomed them, even cultivated them. They had proven a valuable source of story ideas, sort of a subconscious Commonplace Book. But tonight his dreams were unpleasantly vague, redolent of portentous but hidden mysteries of which only hints were revealed. Howard felt as if he were drifting in the deep. Not like a drowning man, but like a submarine camera eye. There were the standard sea-bottom corals and reeds, with anemone and crustaceans. Fish passed him. He had not given a very close look to the fish he had bought and eaten, but he thought that some of these resembled it.

The strangest thing was the haunting *sound*. He had read that whales sing to one another under the waves, but fish? Well, it was only a dream after all. Next he became aware of his breathing and noticed with a start that he was taking in water and draining the oxygen out of it. It felt simultaneously terrifying and familiar. And just before waking up, he saw materializing amid the rippling and shifting waters a weathered and barnacled stone arch framing an ancient metal bell. Currents made its clapper strike the sides and send forth a muffled echo. It was subtle, hard to hear, and yet it woke Howard up like an alarm clock.

He rose from his bed, turned on the lamp, and reached for pencil and paper. He noted what he could recall of the dream. He would study it in the morning and see if it might offer any story possibilities. Maybe a poem. If it proved fruitful, he might send the result around to a few of his Amateur Journalism pals, perhaps Cannon, Gafford, Mariconda. They were honest critics and always offered helpful suggestions. It was Gafford, for instance, who had persuaded him to drop that idea for a story making Negroes the unwholesome spawn of Nyarlathotep.

*

The next time the fish peddler came round, Lovecraft did not know it till it was too late, for his aunt Annie answered the door. She readily agreed to a purchase, a larger one than her nephew had made a couple of weeks before. He must have developed a new fondness for seafood, so she thought she was doing him a favor. When Howard learned of it, he took the news with a grateful smile. It was his own fault. And it couldn't hurt to do a bit more dietary experimentation.

That evening, he was surprised to find three different plates of seafood, none of it familiar. The fish monger certainly offered a varied menu of exotica, for Howard knew he had never seen the like of these breaded and fried creatures. One type reminded him of spiders, albeit with ten legs apiece, and fleshy webs (now crispy) between them. Another variety looked mostly like a large shrimp or crawfish, but with the head of a fish. It had an expression that no fish ought to have. The third looked almost like some abdominal human organ. But it all tasted pretty good! Howard put on the feedbag and afterward apologized for such an unbecoming display of gluttony. For their part, the aunts were glad to see it. Howard had always been too thin.

No gastric disturbance this time, though he did fall asleep much earlier than usual. And he dreamed again. It began very much like the previous dream, but his visions phased in and out between a sea-creature's eye view and that of human swimmers. These latter flashes all climaxed with the sense of sharp pain, claustrophobia, and blackness. With each such vision the pain became more vivid, less dreamlike. Finally the slashing pain awakened him, and he sat bolt upright, covered in cold sweat. And he was sure the perspiration had a salty tang to it.

The next morning, after his first cup of heavily sugar-permeated coffee (few knew it, but Lovecraft had first learned to love coffee flavored ice cream and moved on to the hot drink from there), Lovecraft set aside a fifty-page epistle he had planned to finish, this one to fellow antiquarian Neilly, because he had come up with a story idea based on this latest dream. Suppose a man found himself absorbing the unhuman memories of animals and of fish he had eaten, and then his inherited memories began to draw upon those of human beings whom these animals had devoured…

Lovecraft stopped his creative musings and stared straight ahead. Could this actually *be* what had happened to him? Inheriting memories? He knew of theories of racial memory; he had exploited that in "The Rats in the Walls." He had decided it sounded sufficiently plausible not to make his readers scoff, so he now felt he could allow himself to consider it seriously.

But this sort of thing obviously didn't happen every time anyone had fish for dinner! What was different here? It had to come down to that strange fish peddler. Perhaps he would return and Howard could ask him some questions. And then another idea came to him: he donned his coat, went downstairs, and left the house. For the first time, he knocked on the doors of several of the neighbors on either side of him. He had never met them. Now he introduced himself and asked if any of them had been called upon by a tall, jocose fish peddler. As he had half-expected, none had.

*

Howard continued to write, to take night time walks, and to play with cats he met along the way. They seemed to know to expect him and greeted him with tails straight up. He walked till he felt tired enough to sleep. He would turn in, hoping not to dream. But he did. Most were, thankfully, ordinary dreams. He had not eaten any more fish, thinking it must have inspired the dreams. But a few weeks later he did have another one, another one that seemed more than a dream.

He again found himself swimming through the ocean deep. But this time there was no shifting between perspectives. It was a consistent stream of consciousness. He felt he occupied a larger physical form, larger than in the earlier dreams, larger even than his own waking body. Before, he could not get a look at his body as it glided through the water, but now he saw "his" stroking arms as "he" swam. The skin was leathery, scaled. Some type of diving suit?

But now he, or his dream vehicle, was nearing a large seabed structure. In a moment he could see, as he passed over it, a large roofless hall in which a stooped, frail figure sat before a great many like himself, only younger and larger. From the old one's hand gestures, Howard surmised he was lecturing the others, perhaps his students. He managed a good look at them. If the one whose eyes he shared was wearing a diving suit, so were they. All of them.

He drifted by this scene and on to another. Again, no roof. What need of it down here? To keep the rain out? He saw a great room with a number of artisans fashioning intricate jewelry and other decorative pieces: bracelets, crowns, and pectorals. All bore the likenesses of strange aquatic creatures— including some of those Howard had recently dined on.

A third enclosed area resembled a vast corral, but nothing within it reminded him of any earthly cattle. There he saw rows and rows of shimmering, fluctuating masses of unstable jelly. Like gigantic amoebas, they projected pseudopods and bobbing eyestalks. Manlike figures walked among these creatures, as if tending them, scaly giants like those he had observed in the "lecture hall."

He was gliding toward more buildings in this fantastic undersea metropolis. There was, at the center of the complex, a great fortified castle. The confusing angles of the walls reminded him of Riemannian geometry, something purely theoretical and supposedly possible only in the gulfs of outer space. And that might as well be where he was for the utter strangeness of it. He began to pass over the open top of the huge fortress, but before he could see what pulsated within— he awoke.

This time Howard fell out of bed. Sprawled on the hardwood floor, he propped himself up on his elbows. He stared straight ahead, baffled as to what he should do, what on earth he *could* do next.

Lovecraft was in no measure surprised the next afternoon when a knock came at the door. He sprang from his desk chair and rushed down the stairs, hoping to beat his aunts to the door. But neither was in evidence. Alone, he opened the door. He had already glimpsed the top of the fish monger's head through the fanlight.

There he stood, this time with no fish (or whatever they were) in his huge hands. Howard only now noticed the bumpiness of the grey-green skin, as well as the protuberant eyes. Or perhaps the man had changed in appearance since that first visit.

"Well?"

The man's voice seemed deeper, coarser. "Mr. Lovecraft, we're ready for you."

"What do you mean, sir? Ready for what? I don't understand you."

"You don't have to just dream anymore."

It seemed to Howard that the figure before him, already very tall, grew like a lengthening shadow, becoming more than a single figure, as if to embody decision and destiny waiting for him to take his webbed hand and walk away into another world. Lovecraft had long chafed at the stultifying bonds of the feeble human senses and the ironclad laws of nature, so stingy with her coveted secrets. He had resigned himself to the false and fantasized escapes of the imagination. But here was an opportunity truly to defy those confining bands.

But there was Providence, with its gambrel roofs, its sunset terraces, its narrow, winding lanes and overhanging second stories, the fanlights and harbor whistles, brick warehouses transfigured by the winter sun. Could eternity be better than this? Could its wonders be superior?

Lovecraft slammed the door and went back upstairs.

*

A few days later, Howard met a group of his friends at a favorite restaurant. He was late arriving, and when he pulled out the chair they had saved for him, he smiled and waved hello to his comrades. Michaud was there, and Eckhardt, the artist of dubious reputation in wholesome circles, plus the stalwarts Murray and McNamara, Burleson and Werba, even Selby and Price. All faces he was so glad to see, perhaps now more than ever.

But then his eyes fell upon the repast they were sharing, the so-called "Fisherman's Bounty." With a grimace he ceased his descent to the chair bottom and stepped away.

"You can eat that God-damned stuff if you want, but I'm headed across the street for some ice cream!"

PETER CANNON

"A Providence Pal's Tale"

One day in the fall of 1975, the friend with whom I shared an apartment on Manhattan's Upper West Side, where I had recently moved to seek a career in book publishing, pointed out a notice in the *New York Times* about a forthcoming convention in Providence, R.I., devoted to H. P. Lovecraft. I realized at once this was an event I had to attend.

At this point, other than Professor Barton L. St. Armand, under whose guidance I had written my master's thesis on Lovecraft the year before at Brown, I knew no one who shared my enthusiasm for the work of my favorite horror writer.

In Providence that Halloween weekend, I briefly encountered a number of people who would later play major roles in my Lovecraftian life, notably Frank Belknap Long, HPL's best friend, and Ben Indick, who bought *The Outsider and Others* when it was first published and who kindly signed his essay "Lovecraft's Ladies" in my program book.

But the most important person I connected with that weekend was Professor Dirk Mosig, then perhaps the world's leading Lovecraft scholar. Encouraged by Dirk, I eventually joined the Esoteric Order of Dagon amateur press association, in which I circulated a rather drab-looking photocopied and stapled zine called *Selected Scribblings*.

The Second World Fantasy Convention was held in Manhattan in 1976. Using my badge from the First WFC, I was able to slip into the dealers' room, where I spotted a young fellow at a table full of mimeographed materials by or about Lovecraft. Such was my introduction to Marc Michaud of Necronomicon Press. I was soon a loyal customer.

The following year, I received a letter from someone named S.T. Joshi inviting me to contribute to an essay collection he was compiling, what became *Four Decades of Criticism*, his first published tome. I assumed this gentleman was a college professor, so was duly surprised when I finally learned he was a high school student. S. T. later invited me to contribute articles to *Lovecraft Studies*, and would encourage me in my pursuit of the contract for the Lovecraft volume in Twayne's U.S. Authors series.

In 1978, through a mutual friend who worked at Crown, the publisher where I finally found full-time employment, I met T.E.D. Klein, the author of "The Events at Poroth Farm" (the story that would provide the basis for Ted's first novel, *The Ceremonies*) and a near neighbor on the Upper West Side.

I returned to Providence in 1979 for the Fifth WFC, and in 1980 attended the first of the Lovecraft-related weekends at Roger Williams College in Bristol, R.I. There I had the pleasure of meeting Jason Eckhardt, whose artwork for Necronomicon Press I greatly admired. To my delight, Jason would illustrate much of my work in future years, starting with my Lovecraft-inspired novella, "The Madness out of Space."

Others I met during this period who would become friends and colleagues include Bob Price, Sam Gafford, Steve Mariconda, Ken Faig, and Stefan Dziemianowicz. Such associations can have some unexpected benefits. In particular, I am eternally grateful to Stefan for recommending me to the head of the reviews department at *Publishers Weekly*, the book industry magazine that has employed me as its mystery reviews editor since 2000.

This century a full-time job and a full-time family have meant less time for Lovecraft, but today I regularly go to the New Kalem dinners hosted every couple of months or so by Derrick Hussey, the founder of Hippocampus Press, at an Irish pub in Midtown Manhattan. And I take immense satisfaction in seeing a new generation of fans and scholars following in the footsteps of the pals, even as Lovecraft has grown over the decades from the literary idol of a devout few to world-class author and pop culture phenomenon.

"Zinetime: Or, Fanzines Are Forever"
By Peter Cannon

James Bond stood in front on the unimposing brick building, contemplating the grim task ahead of him. M's orders had been simple enough on the surface: seek out and destroy a secret organization based in New York rumored to be a more deadly threat to the civilized world than SPECTRE. Their name: "The New Kalems." The Kalems had some vague sinister outfit known as the EOD, intelligence reports had surmised; but one thing was certain; they were a bunch of fanatical weirdos. Of course, he'd kill if he had to. To this purpose Bond clutched a time-bomb mechanism, cleverly contrived to resemble a batch of British amateur press journals.

Through a New Jersey religious cultists who put out a speculative periodical full of subversive theological theories, 007 had learned of the meeting that Saturday afternoon, held at the East Seventies apartment of a famed fantasy author-editor. He took a final glance at his disguise—short-sleeved East Anglia University sweatshirt, chino pants, and black high-top sneakers—reflected in the window of the dog grooming salon on the ground floor, then strode inside and pressed the buzzer to 2B. When the intercom crackled, he announced his alias— Guy Cowlishaw, of Bognor Regis.

A skinny chap with brushed-back gray hair, goatee, and oversized glasses greet him at the door of the flat. "Welcome, sir, welcome," said his presumed host, taking Bond's hand in a limp grip and looking fixedly at a point several inches to the right of the spy's elbow.

"Say, could you spare ten bucks? We're kind of low on

supplies. Those Kalems eat like barbarians, heh-heh."

Bond knew panhandlers were endemic to New York, but had scarcely expected to be hit up in this manner. Nonplussed, he forked over a ten-dollar bill. Ring it up to the British taxpayer!

"Thank you kindly, my dear sir, you are a true gentleman," chortled the thin man, as he slipped by Bond and down the stairs.

"You all must be Guy Cowlishaw, of Bognor Regis," exclaimed a younger, plumper chap, also bearded, whose eyes danced with a satanic gleam and whose fingers worked in queer, almost inhuman fashion. "Come on in and meet the gang. Hoo-boy!"

Bond stepped into the comfortable living room, furnished with fireplace, bookshelves, and sleek cat, where he was introduced to several young men, nearly all of them bearded and paunchy. He had clearly joined, to his dismay, a stag gathering. (Bloody hell, just because he was older didn't mean he couldn't get assigned to the more glamorous cases the way he used to...)

"You must be thirsty," said his devilish companion, "how about something to drink?"

Bond indicated his preference for a dry martini.

"A what? Sheesh, I'm sorry, Guy, but all we have in the alcohol department is some white wine... Oops, sorry about that, we've run out—but ole 'Yakthoob' should be back shortly with a new jug. Help yourself to some food in the meantime, though."

Bond surveyed without much enthusiasm a table by the window, laden with assorted soft-drink bottles, potato chip and pretzel fragments, depleted packages of doughnuts, cookies, and other sugary fare. So much for my diet, thought Bond, seizing a couple of Mallomars.

England's most illustrious secret agent took a seat on the couch next to a dignified-looking Indian fellow, who to Bond's mind evoked at least a touch of the old Empire, a reminder of home, amongst the sea of crass Americanism he now found himself wallowing in. The Indian was discussing with a clean-cut, unbearded young man (the only one in the room) some fine philosophical points in the work and thought of the great American horror writer, H. P. Lovecraft. They were soon, however, drowned out by others in the party, who were more inclined to talk about the blood-and-guts antics of Robert E. Howard and his character Conan. Having read both Lovecraft and Howard as part of his training preparation, Bond definitely favored the latter. Howard always had plenty of macho action and well-built babes in his stories, while that milquetoast Lovecraft took aeons to build up to a punch and barely had any females at all in his fiction, let alone any attractive ones.

Bond's mind began to wander—till he noticed that some of the lads who were also disinclined to converse were perusing the magazines on the coffee table. Curiously, upon inspection, they all featured photos of naked black women.

"I've got a weakness for brown sugar," confessed the skinny older guy, who'd returned with a sack of groceries and wine. Well, 007 liked "brown sugar" too. He thought back fondly to one of his adventures in the Caribbean. "Man, was that chick hot in the sack last night," continued their host. "She took one look at my basket..."

There ensued a jolly round of lewd stories and jokes. Eventually, after several glasses of Almaden Chablis, Bond lurched his way toward the cat-scented bathroom. He took the opportunity to study closely the unusual artwork hanging on the walls: color drawings of roughly humanoid extraterrestrials with massive genitals, engaged in what was presumably sex. Weird, mused Bond, pretty weird.

Bond considered leaving the explosive fanzines in the cat box, but maybe that was a little too extreme. After all, he realized by now that special branch had been mistaken: the New Kalems were obviously on the whole a harmless lot. Still, he hadn't come across the Atlantic simply to waste his time. There were other, more subtle ways to take care of them...

Soon after the fateful meeting, the consequences of Bond's behind-the-scenes sabotage became evident. "Yakthoob" abandoned his Manhattan abode for New Jersey exile—a mortal blow to the group. A year later the cultist left New Jersey for the backwoods of North Carolina, and the New Kalems were dead forever. Bond had scored another triumph.

SAM GAFFORD

I first discovered Lovecraft during High School when I found a volume of his short stories in the school library. I'd never heard of him before and honestly thought that the name must be some sort of joke. I took that book home and must have read it about five times before bringing it back. I quickly devoured everything written by Lovecraft that I could find and his work would become one of the major influences in my life and own writing.

But I was alone.

No one I knew had ever even heard of Lovecraft much less read him. I had all of this built-up energy about Lovecraft and his work but no one to talk to about it. I was a cult of one... until I found the Providence Pals.

After discovering the magazine, *Lovecraft Studies*, I'd corresponded with its editor, S.T. Joshi, and he invited me to come visit him in Providence and attend a 'Providence Pals' gathering. That he would open up his home to me and include me in this august group was amazing to me. I'd never known such kindness and largesse. My train ride from Connecticut to

Rhode Island that first time echoed Lovecraft's own return to Providence after his New York Exile.

In that first visit, I met S.T., Marc Michaud, Jason Eckhardt, Bob Price and his wife, Ken Neily and Don Burleson along with his soon to be wife, Mollie. I was welcomed as if I were a new family member. I will never forget that feeling of acceptance and friendship I received then and still receive today almost thirty years later.

That meeting, and my induction into the Providence Pals informal 'gang', remains one of the pivotal events in my life. Because of that meeting, I have gone on to write and publish fiction and articles and essays about weird fiction and many other things. None of which I would have done had I not received that support and encouragement from this group.

As time grew on, more members would join the group and I'd meet Peter Cannon, Steve Mariconda, Will Murray, Bob Knox and others. The spirit of Lovecraft bound us together in a brotherhood that defies explanation. In this company, I would explore Providence and many other Lovecraftian sites in New England, I'd meet Frank Belknap Long and enjoy hearing his stories about Lovecraft as he knew him, I'd be a witness to massive strides in Lovecraft scholarship and criticism and share so many laughs and good times that I truly could not name or count them all.

There are few moments in one's life that can be pointed at and say, "There! That moment changed my life". As a young teenager, I could have gone in different directions. With the "Providence Pals", I found a group of people who encouraged my literary inclinations and showed me a new path I hadn't considered before.

Through the years, we've drifted apart geographically but not spiritually. These are friendships that surpass the miles. Years may go by between our gatherings but, when they do happen, it is as if time has stood still and we are all standing once again in Prospect Terrace looking out over the city that Lovecraft adored and being, now and forever, "Providence Pals".

PASSING SPIRITS
By Sam Gafford

For H.P.L.

"...Cthulhu never existed. Azathoth never existed. Nyarlthotep, Nodens, Shub-Niggurath, Dagon, none of them. I made them all up."

I was sitting in H. P. Lovecraft's small study, listening to him rant. It was 1937. In barely under a year he would be dead of stomach cancer. I felt a need to try to tell him this. To let him know that the pain in his abdomen was not just 'gas' but a serious medical problem that he should seek treatment for immediately. When I tried to explain that I knew all about those types of things, he refused to listen and went on ranting.

"But you know what is the worst thing about all of this?" he continued in his nasal voice. "This is what I'll be remembered for...if I'm remembered by anyone. For making up a pantheon of monster-gods. Basically, for stealing from Dunsany."

I tried to explain that that wasn't the truth. That he had added much more to it than just the idea of a cosmic mythology, but he wouldn't listen. It was very strange and not at all the type of conversation I had envisioned having. I wouldn't say that the man was bitter, but he certainly wasn't happy about a lot of things.

Looking at him, I felt that there were so many things that I should be saying but I didn't. My time was too short for that and the memory was already fading.

When I awoke, I was in my apartment and there was a ribbon of spit on the pillow next to me. I checked it for blood but it was clear. My head throbbed as usual and I felt the familiar dull ache behind my eyes. I crawled out of bed and turned the TV on as I dressed. CNN was going on about some flare up in the Middle East (I had long ago stopped caring about such things, there was always a flare up somewhere or other) and I flipped it over to "Scooby-Doo" on the Cartoon Network. It was one of my favorites from the first year (the best year before they got into all that guest star nonsense and then brought in Scrappy-Doo--who the hell ever thought that was a good idea?) with the laughing space ghost that had the glowing, skull head. I remember how that scared the piss out of me as a kid. A lot of things scared me back then, before I learned that the only real scary thing in life was stuff like cancer and brain tumors. There weren't any gods or monsters. Not in the real world. Here we had sickness and disease instead of vampires and ghosts.

I brushed my teeth and took my medicine. Looking at the clock, I had about an hour to get to work so I knew I'd have enough time. I sat down and watched the rest of the show, waiting for that great 'Scooby-Doo' ending where they unmask the villain. I always loved that.

At work, I tried to pretend that I cared about what I was doing, but it didn't really matter. I was just another clerk in just another bookstore. Nothing special. Nothing unique. I had 'Help Desk' duty which everyone knew was the worst. Listening to blue haired old ladies trying to describe what they wanted. "I don't know the name but I saw it on Oprah. It had a green cover."

The other clerks tried not to look at me too closely. My hair had grown back, more or less, but there's still something about a cancer patient that sets you off from everyone else. Maybe it's a smell or some invisible 'early-warning' system but no one looks at you the same way afterward. That didn't bother me too much. Most of them weren't worth knowing anyway; weird, trendy people of questionable sexuality. I'd never had much in common with them, nor they with me.

Lovecraft's ghost followed me through the Reference section while I guided a customer, pointing out books with errors in them. I hate it when he does that.   "The   tumor's getting larger," intoned Dr. Lyons with all the seriousness of a hanging judge. He held up two Cat Scans. "As you can see from the earlier one, it was only about the size of a grape. Now it's getting close to a plum."

I'd never eaten a plum so had no idea about its size. I figured that it wasn't a good comparison.

"So none of the treatments have done anything?"

Dr. Lyons sighed. "No. The radiation treatments barely seemed to slow its growth. Since we stopped doing those, it's gotten bigger. The medication doesn't seem to be working either. Surgery, although not recommended, is still an option."

"You told me before that it was too dangerous."

"It is. But I don't really see any other way." He got up from behind his desk. "Michael, you have to understand that without surgery this is going to continue to grow."

Apparently I wasn't impressed enough by this.

"Michael, you will die without this operation."

I thought about this. Dying wasn't necessarily the worst thing. Chemo was certainly on an equal footing. Poverty was right up there too.

"How long?"

"If the tumor continues to grow at this rate, maybe 4-6 months, on the outside. But, Michael, they won't be comfortable months."

He went on to describe how, as the tumor grows, I would begin to lose brain functions. My speech and sight would be affected. My coordination would deteriorate and I would start having hallucinations. In short, it would be a living death.

I thanked him and left. Dr. Lyons was confused and followed me out into the hall. He wanted to know why I didn't want to schedule the operation immediately. I looked at him.

"Because I can't afford it." I turned away. He didn't stop me.

Robert E. Howard made a writing career out of stories of strong rugged men who tamed their worlds and bent others to their will. It was a universe of barbarians with strong sword arms and evil sorcerers who plotted magic schemes of conquest. Not once do I recall a REH character dying of cancer or an illness. Of course, that probably would have been too personal a thing considering how his mother died.

"Don't forget," Lovecraft said, "Two Gun Bob killed himself."

"Yeah, well, there's plenty of ways to do that. Sometimes doing nothing works just as well." I replied.

There had been an article in the paper not too long ago about a doctor doing work on cancer treatment. It wasn't one of those peach-pit things but it was an herbal remedy. Supposedly some type of combination of herbs and diets. I'd read a lot of those books including the one by Norman Cousins. Sometimes they seemed to work, most times they didn't. I'd never had the discipline to see them all through but, considering the alternatives, I didn't have a lot of choices.

At work, I looked up the doctor's book. To my surprise, we actually had a copy. Glancing through it, it looked more like a cookbook than anything else. The medicine was a blend of herbs and vitamins (supposedly available at any health food store) and there was a special diet that focused on macrobiotics and avoided things like meat and oils. It seemed to be typical stuff but the doctor's photo had a kind and gentle face so I bought it. I enjoyed making my manager nervous when she rang it up. It was obvious why I was buying it, but no one dared to mention it.

"You know," Lovecraft said to me in a horrified whisper, "someone once said that my Shub-Niggurath was a representation of sexual disease. Can you believe that?"

I heard this at least once a day. It was one of the things that really bothered him given his upbringing and personality.

"Yeah, I can believe it," I replied. My manager didn't even look at me. She had gotten used to me talking like this.

On the way home, I bought the herbs listed in the book at the only local health food store. I didn't recognize most of the names and the clerk wasn't much help either. Several of the ingredients weren't there so I had to substitute. The clerk thought that the other herbs and vitamins were just as good and, even though I didn't believe him, didn't have anything else to go on.

I stopped at a local restaurant and had a big steak meal with a plateful of french fries. My farewell to meat. I avoided the seafood platter out of deference to Lovecraft, who, as always, kept looking around and exclaiming, "Gad, these birds do eat!"

At home later, I read through the book some more. The doctor believed that the steady use of his herb/vitamin combination, along with the diet, was able to curb the growth of cancer. In a few instances he described, the cancer had disappeared completely. I laid the pill bottles on the counter. I mixed the herbs together. There was a specific pattern on what to take, how much, and when. I took the first dose and followed it with Dr. Lyon's medication. It had a long clinical name that I couldn't pronounce but it was "the latest in cancer treatment". Couldn't hurt to keep taking it, I'd paid for it, after all, and it hadn't been cheap; the cost of being poor and sick in America.

There wasn't much on TV that night. The cable channels were all boring so I put an old NIGHT STALKER tape on and read for a while. Out of habit, I picked up THE DUNWICH HORROR and started reading "The Shadow over Innsmouth" again. It had always been one of my favorites but Lovecraft wouldn't give me any peace.

"Disease, disease, disease. That's all they keep talking about. According to some critics, everything I wrote came from a fear of disease, either sexual or mental. Why couldn't it just be a story? Why did it have to be *about* something?"

"You think that's bad," I replied, "you should read Hodgson. Now there's a man who had a real problem with disease."

That piqued his interest and he settled down with a volume of Hodgson's short stories. One of the small press books, of course, I would never have been able to afford a first edition and he wasn't reprinted often.

Lovecraft read quickly and quietly. Reading was one of the few things that kept him calm. Every so often he would chuckle to himself or make a satisfied sound after reading a particularly good section.

In this wise, I eventually fell asleep.

I was walking through the streets of Innsmouth. Past the Esoteric Order of Dagon church (with its sinister shadow in the basement), along the streets of houses that, though habitable showed no signs of life. I walked by the supermarket and waved to the stock clerk who, as usual, bore a striking resemblance to Frank Belknap Long. (I hoped he'd had an easier life than the real Long.) Zadok Allen was wandering about, of course, and we exchanged laughs and old stories.

"Well, ya know, death's funny. It comes when ya don't call and never answers when ya do!" Zadok laughed without the trademark Yankee accent.

Lovecraft the narrator came lumbering down the street from the supermarket and Zadok staggered off to meet him, practicing his Yankee-speak as he walked. They had an appointment to keep.

I sat on the beach and looked out at Devil's Reef. It was an ugly thing; a piece of rock jutting out of the water. Beyond it, I knew, the ocean floor fell away and the Deep Ones swam not far beyond.

Several fishermen with the 'Innsmouth look' stopped by and encouraged me to swim out. "G'wan," they said, "why not?"

Why not, indeed? I took off my clothes (never self conscious in dreams...I had never had the 'waking up in school naked' dream) and entered the water. Though I had done it a few times before, I'd never swum out very far. This time felt different. The water was warmer, heavier than before and it enveloped me like nothing I had ever felt. I swam out to the rock and climbed on top of it.

From there, I could see Zadok and Lovecraft talking on the beach as Zadok gave his little speech. And then it struck me. Every other time I'd been here, I had only seen and experienced what Lovecraft had written in the story. I'd never been out to Devil's Reef before and, remembering the story, neither had the narrator. Oh sure, he described planning on going to Devil's Reef with his cousin and diving off the deep end, but it wasn't an actual place visited in the story. Yet I was there. I could feel the rough stone beneath my fingers and, looking over the other end, could swear that I could see other things beneath the surface, beckoning to me.

Slowly, I dipped into the water and followed.

When I woke up this time, there was blood on the pillow. That wasn't good. I touched my nose and my fingers came away bloody. Suddenly, my head was shoved into an invisible vise and I collapsed back into my pillow, barely able to keep from screaming.

In his chair, stroking an invisible cat that wasn't there but was anyway, Lovecraft sat silently.

After a few minutes, the pain subsided and I was able to sit up. The front of my undershirt was covered in blood. This hadn't been the first attack, but it was definitely the worst.

"Dr. Lyons said it would only get worse," Lovecraft added unnecessarily.

I ignored him and went to clean myself up.

Sometime later, I made myself some breakfast. I didn't have any of the macrobiotic stuff the book doctor recommended so I made do with eggs and bacon. I'd give up the bad stuff later although I had begun to think that there wasn't any point in giving anything up and that I should just surrender to excesses. Spend the last months of my life carousing from one bar to another, drinking too much, eating bad food, sleeping with anonymous women (assuming I could find some who were willing) and give myself up to the extremes.

Lovecraft looked disapprovingly at me. "I know," I said, "you'd probably prefer if I just sat there quietly and suffered like you did while I eat a can of cold beans and some crackers."

"You could do worse," he said, but I didn't see how.

"I could do a lot better," I said and started to mentally count up the money in my bank account. Just enough for a real large splurge or six months of diminishing capacity. Yeah. Life's great.

"What about the dream?" Lovecraft asked.

I looked at him. I'd grown used to him asking questions at the most inappropriate time for a spirit who shouldn't even be here ("Why are you haunting me anyway? What'd I do to you?") but this was unexpected.

"What dream?"

He looked at me. I knew perfectly well what he meant and he had this habit of looking at me a certain way when I was avoiding a subject. I expected him to hand me a business card someday with "H.P. Lovecraft, Conscience" printed on it. Jiminy Cricket had nothing on him.

"It was a dream, that's all."

He just glared at me. "Here," he finally said, "read this. It might help you understand." He threw a copy of Hodgson's THE GHOST PIRATES at me. I still hadn't figured out how he was able to manipulate objects but my head was hurting too much to wonder about it.

I looked at the book. "I read it already."

"Read it again. You obviously didn't get the connection." He went back and starting petting the cat again. It was an all black kitten whose name, if you dared to mention it in today's PC climate, could get you into a lot of trouble. "All the pigeons come home to roost," I thought.

I took the herb/vitamin potion and chased it with one of Dr. Lyons Miracle Cure. "Good for what ails ya!" I got dressed and left for work. On the way, I found the Hodgson buried deep into my coat pocket. He put it there. I put it there. Didn't matter. It was still there anyway.

When I got to work, I saw Keziah Mason in the occult section, chuckling to herself as she read one of the new age witchcraft books. She certainly didn't look like the young, trendy/sexy girls that are witches in today's movies and TV shows. Brown Jenkin was curling around her feet, looking up at her from time to time with a very hungry shine in his eyes. This was something new. Usually it's just Lovecraft, now other characters were coming to visit.

Poe lived virtually his entire life in poverty. He died in a gutter on a street in Baltimore. That tells you something right there. He never lived to see his work gain the notoriety it deserved. Neither did Lovecraft. Neither did Howard. Is there a pattern here?

The last clear thing I remember from that afternoon at work was waiting on Nyarlthotep. I suppose it was only inevitable. With Keziah and Jenkin about, the Dark Man couldn't be far away. I was running the register when he came up. He put a couple of self help books on the counter (two of those I'M OKAY, YOU'RE OKAY self affirmation kind of things) and started fumbling for his wallet. This struck me as kind of funny as I couldn't imagine Nyarlthotep having a wallet. I wondered what would be inside it. Would he have a driver's license? From where? Kadath maybe? Snapshots of Keziah and Azathoth? Who did he want contacted in case of an emergency? And what was the wallet made out of? I started laughing which made him look up at me. The man was dark. I don't mean just your normal black man. Nyarlthotep was the antithesis of light. Then he smiled and I could smell his breath. It wasn't the stagnating breath of decay like I'd been expecting. It was sweet and cloying. It made you think of hot summer nights when the heat sticks to your skin and you can peel your sweat away in layers. My eyes closed and I went away.

I was in the Miskatonic Library with Lovecraft and Henry Armitage. We were looking at the dead thing that lay on the floor where the guard dog had killed it. The upper body was strange enough but it was below the torso that "sheer phantasy began". Wilbur Whateley had died in his attempt to steal the Necronomicon. "Why didn't he just buy a copy from a book dealer off Ebay or something?" I said. Armitage glared at me.

The game was afoot and I was standing in the open fields of Dunwich. Before me was the farmhouse of the Fryes, the poor, doomed Fryes. It was 3 am but I could see everything as if it was high noon. Even from a distance I could hear their terrified conversation on the phone party line. I saw the trees near the house bend apart as the invisible thing came closer. I had expected it to be something like Godzilla rampaging through downtown Tokyo. That's what happens when you're a child of the media and you grow up watching a genre that consumes itself with such gusto.

I heard the splintering of wood and looked up to see the top of the farmhouse cave in in the middle. The screams were horrible. Within seconds, the house was gone and the thing continued walking through the forest. "The Elmer Fryes had been erased from Dunwich."

I made my way up to Sentinel Hill where the final confrontation would take place. I had walked this route before with Lovecraft/Armitage but this time felt different. I could feel the wind on my face. My body had form and substance where before it was only dust and mist. Sometimes I was Rice. Sometimes I was Morgan. And once, just once, there was a brief time when I could have sworn I was Armitage and I was spraying the spawn of Azathoth with the powder.

Above me there was the usual half face squirming in torment except, this time, it stopped. It looked straight at me, ignoring the other two. "And what do you think you're looking at?" it said before it went back to its part and obligingly disappeared. I almost expected it to say "I'm gonna keep my eye on you" before it left, but it didn't. Afterwards we went back to the circle of terrified townsfolk and Armitage went into his speech. "Watch the skies!" I mouthed behind him. "Watch the skies!" The townspeople looked at me as if perhaps the wrong thing had been sprayed with the powder on the hill.

I regretted not seeing Old Wizard Whateley this trip. He was always a lot of fun to talk to, particularly if you got a few drinks into him.

When I awoke, I was in a hospital bed.

I'd been in them before, of course, so this was no real strange thing to me but it still wasn't a good sign. There was a strong coppery taste in my mouth. I knew that wasn't a good sign either. My finger was hooked into one of those machines and I could hear the heart beat monitor behind me, happily beeping away. (I've always wondered why they put those things just out of your sight. As if watching your heartbeat might make it stop.) I felt weak and worn out. My clothes were gone and I was in the hospital gown. Lovecraft was sitting in the chair near by.

"Can you believe what they've done to my city?" he asked when he saw I was finally awake. "They tore up the bridge. Tore up that historic bridge to make room for more traffic and make the downtown more *scenic*." He pronounced scenic with an extra flourish of sarcasm.

"Where am I?" My bed was encircled by one of those curtains but, due to the lack of noise, I could tell I wasn't in an emergency ward. It was still somewhat light out so I knew it was daytime but I didn't know what day.

"You're in Rhode Island Hospital. It's attached to Jane Brown, you know. I went and looked in at the room where I died. There's a nurses station there now. Everything changes."

I pulled the cord and buzzed for the nurse.

A large woman in a white uniform came a few minutes later. She explained that I had been unconscious for the last few days after I'd come into the emergency room by ambulance. "You've had an attack," she said and Dr. Lyons had me admitted. She'd alert him that I was awake and left the room after giving me some more medication. "Pain killers," she said but she didn't bother to tell me what kind.

Inspector Legrasse walked by my door and waved at Lovecraft. He was dragging along some half crazed swamp dweller behind him.

A little while later, Dr. Lyons came in but he looked an awful lot like Jeffrey Coombs from REANIMATOR.

"Mike," he said.

"Dr. Lyons," I replied in my best Jack Webb voice. "Where's Bill Gannon? I heard he got arrested for wife beating."

He looked at me like I was some sort of test bug. "What?"

"Nothing. A lame attempt at pop culture humor. What am I doing here?"

Dr. Lyons pulled up a chair. "You had an attack."

"What kind of an attack?"

He sat there for a moment, searching for the right words. "You were at work. Do you remember that?"

I nodded yes.

"You were waiting on a customer. He was a black gentleman. In the middle of the transaction you began screaming and yelling for him to leave you alone. In fact, I'm told that you actually said that the man should 'take his old witch away and stop haunting you'. Sound familiar?"

"No. Not at all. I really did that?"

"I'm afraid so. A few of your co-workers tried to get you to calm down but you went into a spasm and blacked out. You've been here for two days."

I tried to concentrate on what he was saying but all I could see were those weird dimensional things from FROM BEYOND circling his head.

"What happened?"

"The tumor is growing. It's pressing on the part of your brain that covers motor functions and memory. I don't know

78

what's happening to it. It almost seems as if something is making it grow faster." He paused for a moment. "Michael, you're experiencing hallucinations."

"Oh?"

"It's not unusual, given the tumors location. But I admit that I didn't think this would happen so quickly."

Dr. Lyons/Herbert West stood up so he would appear more impressive.

"Michael, you need to have the operation."

"We've gone over that before."

"I know. You don't have the money or insurance. But we'll find a way, Michael. You've got to do this."

I looked at him. It was easier to just go along.

"Okay. Sure."

"Good. I've got you set up for the operation in two days. We'll keep you here and keep an eye on you until then. Okay?"

I nodded.

"All right. Just rest easy. I'll be back later."

After he left, I laid there for about ten minutes. Then I got up, got dressed and left. Lovecraft followed me out. No one stopped me. It seemed that no one took any notice of me and I wondered if they saw me at all or if it was just the way things are in Rhode Island.

I took the bus home.

There was only one message on my machine. It was from my boss,

"Michael...um, I'm sorry to have to say this but we're going to have to let you go. I hope you understand. We just can't have any more scenes like today. I know you have problems but, legally, we can't afford the risk. Sorry. We'll mail you your last paycheck. Um...so you don't really need to come back. Okay? Hope everything works out for you. Bye."

I took an extra dose of the herb/vitamin potion and laid down in bed.

"So now what are you going to do?" asked Lovecraft.

I didn't say anything.

Lovecraft was standing near the window. There wasn't much of a view to see. He had on one of his father's old suits. It fit him pretty well but was still a little loose in the shoulders. I wasn't sure if it was one of the suits that got stolen while he was in New York.

"You know," I finally said, "I've read both of the biographies. Joshi and DeCamp's."

He grimaced.

"At least Joshi took the time to try and understand the era," he responded. "DeCamp lived through some of it and he still couldn't understand how it affected me."

"They never said much about your death. About how you felt as you laid there in that bed at Jane Brown."

He turned to look at me. For some reason, his lantern jaw looked more solid. I could almost swear that his chin was reflecting the light.

"Go to sleep, Michael." It was the first time I had heard him refer to me by name.

I went to sleep.

Professor Wilmarth/Lovecraft was talking about the black stone. Akeley had sent it through the mail and it had disappeared. I took out the stone from Machen's "The Novel of the Black Seal" and showed it to him. He was interested but disappointed. "Yes, but it's not quite what we're looking for." He played the record for me and I listened to that strange otherworldly voice.

"To Nyarlathotep, Mighty Messenger, must all things be told. And He shall put on the semblance of men, the waxen mask and the robe that hides, and come down from the world of Seven Suns to mock...."

It was not surprising that it was my voice speaking on the record.

Wilmarth/Lovecraft took no notice.

Suddenly, we jumped forward and I was in Akeley's cabin. Wilmarth/Lovecraft was talking to Akeley who was sitting in the opposite chair and covered in his huge robe.

Akeley was describing Yuggoth with its great cities of black stone. After a while, Wilmarth/Lovecraft went to bed and I took his place.

"So," Akeley said in that queer, disjointed voice, "what are you looking for?"

"Not much," I answered. "It's just that, I've always wondered--a lot of us have wondered--who are you really? Under that mask. Who are you? Are you a Fungi? Are you Nyarlathotep?"

"Why don't you see for yourself?"

I reached over and took off the mask. It was Lovecraft. "Of course," he said, "who else would it be?"

I never developed a taste for Clark Ashton Smith. I knew he was a good writer but just something about his work never clicked with me. Lovecraft, Howard and Smith were touted as Weird Tales "three musketeers". And yet it was often said that Seabury Quinn was more popular with the readers than any of them. Lovecraft never got a cover. Guess Margaret Brundage just couldn't bring herself to paint Cthulhu and, after all, there were no half naked damsels in distress in Lovecraft. Maybe he would have been more successful if there had been.

The next few days passed strangely.

I don't need to say that I didn't show up for the operation. Dr. Lyons called once, demanding to know where I was and why I didn't come in. He didn't call again. In fact, nobody called after a while. I got to the point where I had to pick up the phone and check it regularly to make sure it was still working.

I stopped doing that when a thick, guttural voice came on the empty line and said, "YOU FOOL, WARREN IS DEAD!"

The dreams went back and forth then. Sometimes I'd have them when I was sleeping. Sometimes I'd have them when I was awake. I'd be walking down Thayer Street and suddenly I'd be walking down a street in Arkham, heading for the Witch House.

Were they real? Was anything real at this point? I remember all those stories where everyone knows that the dreams are real except for the dreamer. In PET SEMETARY, the main character (whose name escapes me but he was played by Dale Midkiff in the movie which wasn't a bad adaptation--King had suffered far worse) goes for a midnight walk with the spirit of the dead student. The student leads him down the path to the Pet Semetary and then tells him not to go beyond the wall. He might as well have put a big neon sign saying, "This way to the Wendigo's Zombie grounds". When he wakes up, he's stunned to find his feet covered with mud and sticks. When I read that, I wasn't overcome with fear. Of course the dream was real. Aren't they always? My first thought was, "Damn, that's gonna be hard to clean up."

The dreams. Eventually the dreams are the only thing that's real. In the dreams there's no cancer, only monsters, gods, demons, ghouls and things you can grab and hold with your hands. Something you can fight and batter into submission. Ever try to grab a cancer?

I stopped eating after a while. Didn't know why I was bothering anyway. Everything tasted the same and had that metallic, copper taste to it. Lovecraft approved of that. We talked a long time about things and only occasionally would something creep through the woods or the walls. I kept taking the herb/vitamin potion along with Dr. Lyons medication until it ran out. The Hounds of Tindalos ran through every once in a while but stopped coming when I ran out of food to give them. The cats of Ulthar never bothered to come at all, preferring to stay on the moon until everything was over.

"Am I dying?" I asked Lovecraft.

"Maybe. Who knows? What is death? Don't ask me."

"But you're dead."

"I am?"

I finally found the section in THE GHOST PIRATES that Lovecraft was talking about.

The good ship had been plagued by the appearance of ghost pirates who are making away with the sailors. There were ghost ships following them through the mist. The narrator tries to explain what's happening:

> "'Well, if we were in what I might call a healthy atmosphere, they would be quite beyond our power to see or feel, or anything. And the same with them; but the more we're like this, the more real and actual they could grow to us. See? That is, the more we should become able to appreciate their form of materialness. That's all. I can't make it any clearer.'"

I was spending more time away. I couldn't remember what day it was or what month. The cable was shut off eventually which was okay because the electricity followed shortly after. I laid in bed, fumbling through my mind. Things and places wandered through me until, eventually, I found myself spending less and less time in that small room in Rhode Island. When I was there, my head was one large hurt. I had begun to think of my brain as a big black stain. If I could lift my head and look in the mirror, I felt sure that my eyes would be completely black.

Lovecraft accompanied me most of the time but sometimes I was alone walking through the worlds. I was solid, with form and substance. Here, I was thin and ghostly. The people there welcomed me. They grabbed my hand, slapped me on the back and brought me along. Here, only Lovecraft stayed at my side and, eventually, I woke up and even he wasn't there anymore. He had moved beyond and to see him, I'd have to let myself drift away.

I didn't float off like you hear in those near-death shows. I fell away from myself, sinking through the earth. I was going beyond and following old Joe Slater to that strange place that was a star far away which shined upon Olathoë aeons ago.

The ground below me became a solid deck of a ship. I felt it move through the water as we raced forward into the strange and forbidding water where an island had suddenly appeared.

Asenath looked at me through Edward Derby's eyes. I sent six three bullets into his brain.

I reached for the smooth surface of polished glass.

I thrilled to the sound of Erich Zann's music as the deaf , mute man called to something outside the window.

I tore through Capt. Norrys' body while the sounds of the rats ran off in the distance.

I unfurled the photo at the corner of Pickman's painting.

I cringed in Nahum Gardner's farmhouse as the colour sprang free.

I...I...I... had become... fiction.

STEVE MARICONDA

When I first saw Benefit Street on a spring afternoon, it was surreal to be inside the scene I had read about in "The Shunned House." The dreamlike effect was heightened by the weather and the flat late afternoon light. A very fine mist—not rain, not drizzle, but an aerosol suspension in from Narragansett Bay--hung in the air beneath an even overcast. The sunlight was bright, but there were no shadows. It was a two-dimensional tableau of magnificent Federal wood frame houses whose edges were softened, but whose tones were vivid in colonial yellow, wedgewood blue, forest green, and primrose. The painterly scene was strangely quiet, too, as the mist muffled the remote sounds of traffic.

As wonderful as this was, Providence a few years later was even greater with the Providence Pals. Meeting this cordial and brilliant group of friends was the culmination of "providential" contact with other cordial and brilliant Lovecraftians—first R. Alain Everts by mail, then David E. Schultz by mail and at his home in Milwaukee WI. David put me in touch with the New York City branch—Robert M. Price, S.T. Joshi, and Peter Cannon. These good souls, in turn, invited me to travel with them to the "holy city" of HPL.

Bob was a Baptist minister with multiple Ph.Ds, whose areas of interest spanned from hermeneutics to comic books, who was among the most articulate and interesting persons I ever met. S.T. was a graduate student at Princeton—but also the leading Lovecraft scholar who not only welcomed me, but also graciously shared his hard-won primary research, recruited me as a critic, encouraged me to write, and published my essays. Peter was an editor, a seasoned HPL scholar, who could extend a conversational thread in the most enlightening of ways on HPL's life and letters, down to the most remarkable level of detail.

There were more Pals in up in Providence. I couldn't visit there as often as I would've liked, but the others I met there were possessed of the same largess. Don was a professor of both Mathematics and English, with a twinkle in the eye that may have been from the unrivalled wickedness of his humor or his rabid intellect. And yet he was no match for his wife Molly—it was delightful to see how Lovecraft had bought two truly kindred souls together. In Jason Eckhardt was not only congeniality and sensitivity, but also artistic talent like none I had ever encountered--the greatest weird artist, I realized later, since Virgil Finlay. Sam Gafford was studious, sincere, and welcoming, a good walker and talker about all things weird fiction. Marc Michaud was affable, too, and maybe the bravest of the bunch--persistent, hard working, willing to put it all on the line to publish writing by and about Lovecraft.

From the first I was amazed at the generosity and good fellowship of all the people I was so lucky to meet. They all exhibited *genius* in the varied senses of the word: in superior intellectual ability, surely, but also in creativity, inspiration, and talent. More than this, they possessed genius in the sense defined in Diderot and d'Alembert's *Encyclopédie*: their souls were more expansive, and they were interested by all that is in nature.   We talked not just about Lovecraft but about an amazing range of things.

What I remember most, however, is the laughs. Many aspects of Lovecraft are funny, intentionally and unintentionally. Never did a few minutes pass in this company without some truly hilarious moments.

I'm grateful to know them all.

"As Time Goes on I See a Shadow Coming:"
M. R. James' Grammar of Terror
By Steven J. Mariconda

Writing in Gale's *Dictionary of Literary Biography,* critic William Atkinson makes the seemingly bizarre claim that M. R. James should be considered a literary modernist, "for the modernist movement in all the arts questioned the possibility of unequivocal representation." The vision of the sedate traditionalist James in the company of Gertrude Stein and Pablo Picasso is enough to make one pause, and if not smirk. However, a closer reading of James tends to support rather than refute Atkinson's position. His observation that the stories' "very narratability seems to be in question" hints at the proposition put forth here: that it is by the adroit use of *grammar* that James created his horrors--horrors of past evils that persist to trouble the present.   In particular, we will examine how three interrelated grammatical elements work together in James to help create spectral atmosphere.

- *Tense* is a category of grammar that expresses time reference-- past, present and future. Tenses are usually manifested by the use of specific forms of verbs, particularly in their conjugation patterns. They typically express time reference relative to the moment of speaking (absolute tense) or relative to the moment being spoken about (relative tense).
- *Aspect* is a category of grammar that expresses how an action, event or state (denoted by a verb) relates to the flow of time.

Perfective aspect describes an event conceived as bounded and unitary, without reference to any flow of time. Imperfective aspect is used for situations conceived as existing continuously, or repetitively, as time flows. In particular James uses Imperfective Aspect when describing evils from the past that persist into the present narrative frame.

- Mood is used to express *modality*, which includes such properties as uncertainty, evidentiality, and obligation. Commonly encountered moods include the indicative, subjunctive, and conditional. Subjunctive forms of verbs are typically used to express various states of unreality such as wish, emotion, possibility, judgment, opinion, necessity, or action that has not yet occurred. The subjunctive mood has several uses in dependent clauses--discussing hypothetical or unlikely events, or expressing opinions or emotions.

"It is" or "It was:" Narration in James and LeFanu

The uniqueness of James' approach to narrative grammar first becomes striking when one considers his tales in the context of those of Joseph Sheridan LeFanu. James never failed to promote LeFanu as his exemplar, so one might reasonably conclude he used similar methods. But an inventory of the words the two writers use immediately reflects a divergence. In particular, LeFanu often writes in the past tense, which James often writes in the present tense. James' horrors exist in the here and now.

LeFanu's use of traditional past-tense narrative is implied when James, in a critical article, cites "the victim's dim forebodings of what is to happen gradually growing clearer" as a strength of LeFanu's narration. This is supported by the frequency in LeFanu of the past-tense verb *had*. In James, conversely, we find that the forms *has, be, have, been* and combinations thereof predominate. The marked contrast in the use of verb tense is apparent in these passages, chosen almost at random, which describe strange apparitions. First from LeFanu:

It [the shadow of a figure] <u>was</u> so thrown obliquely that the hands reached to the windowsill, and the feet stretched and stretched, longer and longer as she looked, toward the ground, and disappeared in the general darkness, and the rest, with a sudden flicker, shot downwards, as shadows will on the sudden movement of a light, and <u>was</u> lost in one gigantic leap down the castle wall. ["Ultor De Lacy"]

And from James:

It <u>would stop</u>, raise arms, bow itself towards the sand, then <u>run</u> stooping across the beach to the water, edge and back again, and then, rising upright, once more <u>continue</u> its course forward at a speed that was startling and terrifying. ["Oh, Whistle, and I'll Come to You, My Lad"]

Even in shorter sentences the difference in the use of tense is evident; for example:

James: The account <u>is</u> blunt and terrible. ["Two Doctors"]

LeFanu: The effect of it <u>was</u> powerful. ["The Mysterious Lodger"]

James: There <u>is</u> no chimney. ["Number 13"]

LeFanu: There <u>was</u> no other mode of exit. ["Schalken the Painter"]

With this distinction in mind, a more detailed review of James' work shows that he was innovative not merely in the use of grammatical tense.   In terms of grammatical aspect, James often uses the perfective aspect, which indicates that an event occurred prior to (but has continuing relevance at) the time of reference: "I have seen"; "he had seen"; "you will have guessed." Closer examination of James also shows his pervasive use of various kinds of modality expressing doubt: *much, just, very, almost, considerable, enough, hardly* and the ubiquitous *rather, perhaps,* and *quite.*

In this use of tense, aspect, and modality to create horror—to convey the intrusion of the past into the present or, more generally, to convey the uncanny commingling of temporal realities—James was highly sophisticated and atmospherically effective. This technique was an important influence upon subsequent writers of supernatural fiction, and has been adopted and extended to great advantage by two leading modern exponents, Ramsey Campbell and Thomas Ligotti.

"Forging the Links between Past and Present:" James' Narratology

Introducing his critical edition of James' tales, S. T. Joshi marks the signal achievement of James as follows:

> Where he differed from his predecessors . . .
> was in suggesting the pervasiveness of the
> past's influence upon the present: his tales . . .
> establish a continuity between past and present
> in which the present is entirely engulfed and
> rendered fleeting and ineffectual . . .
> ["Introduction", in CM xii]

Most commentary has naturally focused on the depth of James's antiquarian knowledge as the basis of his ability to evoke terror from history. But elsewhere Joshi astutely notes that notes that James gave great thought and energy to "the mechanics of narrating the ghost story." He necessarily gleans this from internal evidence, as James is famously coy regarding his theory of the weird tale. James at least admits that "[a]n ancient haunting can be made terrible and can be invested with actuality, but it will tax your best endeavors to forge the links between the past and the present in a satisfying way." ["Ghosts—Treat Them Gently;" HDH 262]. He remains silent as to how he himself addresses the challenge, elsewhere noting only that "[I]f a really remote date be chosen, there is more than one way of bringing the reader in contact with it" ["Introduction to *Ghosts and Marvels;*" HDH 248].

"More than One Way:" Grammatical Strategies in James' Narratives

This leaves the interested reader to discover for himself James' methods. In fine, James uses savvy deployment of certain elements of grammar—tense, aspect, and modality—to create his atmosphere of antique horrors malignantly active in the present.

Tense and Aspect

Tense and aspect are separate grammatical systems that work together semantically. Tense has to do with *when* an event or state of being occurred, and indicates the time (as past, present, or future) and the continuance or completion of an action or state of being. Aspect, in contrast, has to do with the *duration* or degree of completeness of an event or state of being. And this is where things get interesting, because James skillfully plays aspectual constructions against tense forms— mixing elements which indicate that (for example) an event began in the past and "bumped up against" a more recent event in the past, or that an event that began in the past continues into the present.

Modality

Modality is grammar that reflects that narrator's attitude about what he says, his degree of certainty regarding statements he makes, and the level of commitment he attaches to his utterances. Specifically, James' tales are laced with what is called epistemic modality, which encompasses the ways in which the narrator indicates his degree of commitment to the truth of propositions, and reflects his level of knowledge or belief. The most common sources of epistemic modality in English are the modal auxiliaries—constructions like *could have been, ought to, would rather, might be.* The vigilant reader will find that it is impossible to read a page of James without encountering a veritable phalanx of these constructions, often moving in contrary epistemic directions. There is also an arsenal of qualifying adverbs--epistemic adverbs (e.g. *perhaps)* expressing uncertainty or possibility; adverbs of duration (e.g. *briefly)* that constrain timeframes communicated by certain aspectual constructions; adverbs of degree (e.g. *somewhat)* that qualify the sense of another word—all these James deploys to create a veritable no man's land of uncertainty regarding the flux of reality—what was, what is, and what should or should not be.

"Some Future Time Which Never Came:" Duration in "Count Magnus"

"Count Magnus" opens with the narrator explaining that he has assembled the tale from disparate sources. It is told largely from the perspective of Mr. Wraxall, an antiquarian who takes as his study a deadly subject— the evil Count Magnus. Wraxall haplessly resurrects the undead count, and is killed for his trouble.

> The deathless state of being possessed by Count Magnus is reflected in the story's grammar, particularly in the use of adverbs of duration (aspect). At the start of the tale James

describes an event (a warehouse fire) completed before another event in a possible future (the narrator's prospective further research on Wraxall).

It is probable that he entertained the idea of settling down at some future time which never came; and I think it also likely that the Pantechnicon fire in the early seventies *must have destroyed* a great deal that *would have thrown* light on his antecedents, for he refers once or twice to property of his that was warehoused at that establishment. [CM 72-3]

Here we see two future perfect constructions (a modal *[must/would]* plus *have* plus a past participle) create a sense of the past embedded in the present.

The sense of uncertainty regarding the integrity of the present as up against the past is also enhanced here as throughout James, by what we can generally call qualifiers-- epistemic adverbs, adverbs of duration, and adverbs of degree:

Certainly, and *perhaps* fortunately in this case, there was neither voice nor any that regarded: only the woman who, *I suppose,* was cleaning up the church, dropped *some* metallic object on the floor, whose clang startled me.

In all his stories James leans heavily--almost intrusively-- on the epistemic adverbs *perhaps* (expressing uncertainty or possibility), *quite* (to a certain extent) and *rather* (to a certain or significant extent or degree).

Because the perfective aspect communicates duration, another type of adverb is needed to focus in on, or bound, the time dimension implied. In the climactic scene in which Wraxall

93

releases Magnus, James uses temporal adverbials to mark how one event—what happened in the tomb—encroaches upon to another event—Wraxall writing his account in the narrative present:

> . . . . I stooped to pick it up, and—Heaven is my witness that I am writing only the bare truth—*before* I had raised myself there was a sound of metal hinges creaking, and I distinctly saw the lid shifting upwards. I may have behaved like a coward, but I could not for my life stay *for one moment.* I was outside that dreadful building *in less time than I can write*—almost *as quickly as I could have said*—the words; and what frightens me yet more, I could not turn the key in the lock. *As I sit here* in my room noting these facts, I ask myself (it was not *twenty minutes ago*) whether that noise of creaking metal continued, and I cannot tell whether it did or not. I only know that there was something more than I have written that alarmed me, but whether it was sound or sight I am not able to remember. What is this that I have done?" [CM 78]

There is a lot happening grammatically in this very adroit and effective passage. Note how the verb tense wobbles between various states of past tense to various states of present tense. Note how some of the perfect constructions—"I may have behaved," "I could have said," (modal plus present perfect); "I am writing" (present perfect progressive); "I have done" (present perfect) require adverbial markers ("for one moment;" "quickly") to delimit the timing of the events. James also uses the participles *noting* (present progressive), *creaking,* and *shifting* (past progressive) to further mark time. The result of mixing past and present tense and several types of aspect is sort of *temporal cohesion* in which the past and present become enmeshed, in the process throttling the doomed Mr. Wraxall.

"Have You Explored it Ever?:" Labyrinthine Tense and Aspect in "Mr. Humphreys and His Inheritance"

In "Mr. Humphreys and His Inheritance" the title character's ancestor has left him a house and property. "There's an old temple, besides, and a maze," says Humphreys' new neighbor. "Really?," Humphreys replies, "Have you explored it ever?' [CM 219]. The present perfect construction "Have you explored it" with the temporal adverbial "ever" awkwardly tacked-on signals trouble ahead. It seems Humphreys' ancestor practiced the dark arts; the maze casts a perpetual ill influence on those who traverse it, apparently because his cremation ashes lie within the decorative globe at the center.

The maze, as critics have noted, may be seen as a metaphor for the text itself. In the narrative James uses mixed verb tenses and aspectual constructions to create a sense of *nested time* in which the past is environed within the present. In one of the most beautifully written and fully realized passages in James, Humphreys' experiences a kind of reverie as he looks out his study window over the property. But note how the verb tenses shift and the aspectual construction become tortuous:

> But *now* the distant woods *were* in a deep stillness; the slopes of the lawns *were* shining with dew; the colours of some of the flowers *could almost be guessed*. The light of the moon *just caught* the cornice of the temple and the curve of its leaden dome, and Humphreys *had to own* that, so seen, these conceits of a past age *have* a real beauty. In short, the light, the perfume of the woods, and the absolute quiet *called up* such kind old associations in his mind that *he went on* ruminating them for a long, long time. As he *turned* from the window he *felt* he *had never seen* anything more complete of its sort. The

one feature that *struck* him with a sense of incongruity was a small Irish yew, thin and black, which *stood* out like an outpost of the shrubbery, through which the maze *was* approached. That, he *thought, might as well be* away: the wonder *was* that anyone *should have thought* it *would look well* in that position. [CM 236]

Having first set the temporal reference point *now,* James zig-zags off into a winding path of modal auxiliaries (i.e., *could almost be guessed, had to own, might as well be, should have thought, would look well)* that disorients the reader, much as the demonic maze deranges its fictive occupants.

"I Must be Firm:" Modal Disquiet in "The Stalls of Barchester Cathedral"

"The Stalls of Barchester Cathedral" is one of James' best stories, offering an unusually rich character study of the ill-fated Dr. Haynes, Archdeacon at Barchester Cathedral. James implies at the outset that Haynes had a hand in the accidental death of his predecessor: an unsympathetic character, surely. But as the narrative recounts, from Haynes perspective, how the Archdeacon is set upon by the demonic statues carved on the cathedral stalls, James deftly creates an emotional ambivalence that sets the story apart. Haynes' letter to a magazine asking for help in identifying the carvings offers James the opportunity to indulge himself in a more ornate style than he usually employs:

. . . One [statue] is an exquisitely modelled figure of a cat, whose *crouching* posture suggests with admirable spirit [its] suppleness, vigilance, and craft. . . . Opposite to this is a figure seated upon a throne . . . but it is no earthly monarch whom the carver *has sought to* portray. . . . [N]either the crown nor the cap which he wears suffice to hide the prick-ears and *curving* horns which betray his Tartarean origin; and the hand which rests upon his knee, is armed with talons of *horrifying* length and sharpness. Between these two figures stands a shape muffled in a long mantle. This might at first sight be mistaken for a monk or 'friar of orders gray,'. . . . A slight inspection, however, *will lead to* a very different conclusion. The knotted cord is quickly *seen to be* a halter, held by a hand all but concealed within the draperies. . . . These figures are evidently the production of no unskilled chisel; and should it chance that any of your correspondents are able to throw light upon their origin and significance, my obligations to your valuable miscellany *will be largely increased."* [CM 186-7]

The present tense with interspersed present participles *(crouching, curving, horrifying)*, present perfect *(seen to be)*, and future perfect *(will lead to, will be increased)* constructions paint a vivid tableaux. The use of the present perfect regarding the creator of the statues—"the carver *has sought to* portray;" the "figures *are . . . the production* of no unskilled chisel"--is especially powerful in establishing the feeling the carvings are alive.

But this is exceeded by one of the most uncharacteristically empathetic—one might even say poignant-- passages in James:

After that, as time goes on, I [the narrator] see a shadow coming over him [Dr. Haynes]—destined to develop into utter blackness—which I cannot but think must have been reflected in his outward demeanour. He commits a good deal of his fears and troubles to his diary; there was no other outlet for them. He was unmarried and his sister was not always with him. But I am much mistaken if he has told all that he might have told. A series of extracts shall be given: . . . . [CM 187-8]

In this brief but remarkable paragraph, the oscillating tense and aspect connote a narrator ruminating regretfully with himself over what was, what is, and what might have been—with the past and present again meshed into a single locus of fear:

- *After* that
- *[A]s time goes on*
- I *see* a shadow *coming* over him.
- [It is] destined *to develop* into utter blackness.
- I *cannot* but *think* [it].
- [It] must *have been* reflected in his outward demeanour.
- He *commits* a good deal of his fears to his diary.
- There *was* no other outlet for them.
- He *was* unmarried.
- His sister *was* not always with him.
- I *am* much mistaken.
- He *has* told all.
- He *might have* told [all].

In the abrupt final modal phrase *shall be given,* is it as if James pulls himself up sharp by choosing the passive verb form and the modal *shall* (evoking a sense of obligation) so as to prevent his emotions from further intruding into the narration.

Subsequent passages of excellence in this story also show James using tense and aspect to advantage. When Haynes' hand upon on the cat carving feels wet fur, the past tense, past perfect, and present participle are concatenated to create an instant of real terror: "The impression of the unpleasant feeling *was* so strong that *I found* myself *rubbing* my hand upon my surplice" [CM 188]. But the horror becomes most intense near the end when the Archdeacon, who has been shadowed by what hopes to be a common domestic cat, more or less breaks down syntactically:

> A nervous man, which I am not, and hope I am not becoming, would have been much annoyed, if not alarmed, by it. The cat was on the stairs to-night. I think it sits there always. There *is* no kitchen cat. [CM 191]*

This passage is genuinely unnerving, seeming as it does to show the splintering of a psyche from fear. We may note the loose grammatical parallels with the prior narrative exposition in this tale cited above, which strengthen the uncanny effect.

I *hope.*	I *see.*
I am not *becoming*	A shadow [is] *coming.*
I *would have been* annoyed.	[It] *must have been* reflected.
It *sits* there.	He *commits* a good deal of his fears to his diary.
The cat *was* on the stairs.	There *was* no other outlet for them.
There *is* no cat.	I *am* much mistaken.
I *am not* [a nervous man].	He *has told* all.
I *am not becoming* [a nervous man].	He *might have told* [all].

The nature of the ghost story—its need to consider the possible reality of the supernatural—causes *epistemic modality* (regarding attitudes of knowledge and belief) to take center stage in James. There are other flavors of modality, however, one of which is deontic. Deontic modality manifests when the narrator has to order, or promise, or place an obligation on someone. The modal *must* expresses *necessity*, and the protagonist/victim of "The Stalls of Barchester Cathedral" has an intense necessity to escape from the demonic carvings.

> These words, *I must be firm,* occur again and again on subsequent days; sometimes they are the only entry. In these cases they are in an unusually large hand, and dug into the paper in a way which *must have broken* the pen that wrote them. [CM 193]

As Dr. Haynes *must be* firm, so *must have* the pen broken. Unfortunately for the Doctor, those modals that express the *strongest sense of obligation* in deontic mode are the modals that also express *the strongest likelihood* in epistemic mode [Berk 135]. So for our purposes:

I *must be* firm = Those *must not be* demonic carvings.

But apparently they were. Or are.

"Strangely Unobservant He Must Have Been:" Epistemic Architecture in "Number 13"

One of James' most amusing stories is also one of his slightest: "Number 13," set in a Denmark hotel. It uses a familiar trope—a ghostly room that sometimes exists, sometimes not. The occupants of collocated rooms hear someone acting silly in the chamber that should be on the other side of their respective walls. But there is no Number 13, only a ghost space occupied by a ghost who apparently sold his soul to the devil and having a great time for it.

The story is basically a now-you-see-it-now-you-don't shell game, with James remodeling the building using mere grammar when the protagonist isn't looking. When the latter first arrives, he has to choose a room:

> Either Number 12 or Number 14 *would be* better, for both of them looked on the street. . . . Eventually Number 12 was selected. [CM 55]

Either Number 12 or Number 14 *would be* better, indeed, because unlike Number 13 they exist in the present perfect. Number 13 exists in some other realm of entity.

But there is something deeply suspect, too, about the occupant of the adjacent room. The narrator reveals his degree of uncertainty with a number of modal adverbs and the modal auxiliary *must be possessed* and *must be flickering:*

> He *seemed* to be a tall thin man—or was it *by any chance* a woman?--at least, it was someone who covered his or her head with *some kind of* drapery before going to bed, and, he thought, *must be possessed* of a red lamp-shade—and the lamp *must be flickering* very much. There was a distinct playing up and down of a dull red light on the opposite wall. He craned out a little to see if he could make any more of the figure, but beyond a fold of some light, *perhaps* white, material on the window-sill he could see nothing. [CM 56]

The petty annoyances of the traveler escalate as the protagonist misplaces his suitcase. But the suitcase suddenly reappears: "How it *could possibly have* escaped him the night before he did not pretend to understand; at any rate, *there it was now* [CM 57].* The linking of *there it was* and the reference point *now* indicates that the traveler is in an uncanny temporal space, where past and present have an unwholesome relation. The next morning it gets worse: the future perfect has bumped up against a past-passive modal: "Another shock *awaited* him. Strangely unobservant he *must have been* last night" [CM 57].

Complaints to the landlord only incite abuse, and the use of the past progressive--"he *was becoming* quite nervous about the question of the existence of Number 13" [CM 60]--reflects the protagonist's escalating sense that the building's history is an active, present danger.

James uses the reported speech of the landlord to jumble grammar in a yet more threatening way:

> "My Number 13? Why, *don't I tell you* that *there isn't such a thing* in the house? I thought *you might have noticed* that. If *there was it would be* next door to your own room." "Well, yes; only *I happened to think*—that is, *I fancied* last night *that I had seen* a door numbered thirteen in that passage; and, really, *I am* almost certain *I must have been* right, for *I saw it* the night before as well." Of course, Herr Kristensen *laughed* this notion to scorn, as Anderson *had expected,* and emphasized with much iteration the fact that no Number 13 *existed* or *had existed* before him in that hotel. [CM 60]

As we read these sentences, and follow the oscillating movements of grammatical tense, aspect, and modality, we can sense time itself flickering in a manner far more sinister than the neighbor's red lamp.

NOTE

*Note the constructional similarity of "I think it sit there always" ("The Stalls of Barchester Cathedral") and "there it was now" ("Number 13") with "Have you explored it ever?" from "Mr. Humphreys and His Inheritance." The oddly appended temporal adverbials in these examples create a sense of unnatural duration.

BIBLIOGRAPHY

Atkinson, William. "M. R. James." In The Dictionary of Literary Biography, Vol. 156: British Short-Fiction Writers, 1880-1914: The Romantic Tradition. William F. Naufftus, ed. Detroit: Gale Group, 1996, pp. 1780180.

Azar, Betty Schrampfer. Chartbook: A Reference Grammar: Understanding and Using English Grammar. White Plains NY: Pearson Education, 2000.

Berk, Lynn M. *English Syntax: From Word to Discourse.* New York: Oxford University Press, 1999

Comrie, Bernard. Aspect: An Introduction to the Study of Verbal Aspect and Related Problems. Cambridge: Cambridge University Press, 2001.

Huddleston, Rodney. *Introduction to the Grammar of English.* Cambridge: Cambridge University Press,
1984.

Hurford, James R. *Grammar: A Student's Guide.* Cambridge: Cambridge University Press, 1994.

James M. R. *Count Magnus and Other Ghost Stories (The Complete Ghost Stories of M. R. James, Vol. 1).* S. T. Joshi, ed. New York: Penguin Classics, 2005. Cited in the text as CM.

------------. The Haunted Doll's House and Other Ghost Stories (The Complete Ghost Stories of M.R. James,
Vol. 2). S. T. Joshi, ed. New York: Penguin Classics, 2006. Cited in the text as HRH.

Joshi, S. T. "M. R. James." In The Weird Tale: Arthur Machen, Lord Dunsany, Algernon Blackwood, M.R. James, Ambrose Bierce, H. P. Lovecraft. Austin: University of Texas Press, 1990.

Karkkainen, Elise. Epistemic Stance in English Conversation: A Description of Its Interactional Functions. Philadelphia: John Benjamins Publishing Co., 2003

Langacker Ronald W. Foundations of Cognitive Grammar, Vol. II: Descriptive Application. Stanford: Stanford University Press, 1991.

LeFanu, J. S. *Best Ghost Stories of J. S. LeFanu.* New York: Dover Publications, 1964.

--------------. *Ghost Stories and Mysteries.* New York: Dover Publications, 1975.

Phelan, James. Living to Tell About It: A Rhetoric and Ethics of Character Narration. Ithaca: Cornell University Press, 2004.

Prince, Gerald. *A Dictionary of Narratology* (revised ed.). Lincoln: University of Nebraska Press, 2003.

Toulmin, Stephen. *The Uses of Argument.* Cambridge: Cambridge University Press, 1964.

Wardhaugh, Ronald. Understanding English Grammar: A Linguistic Approach. Malden MA: Blackwell, 2002.

WILL MURRAY

To Providence and Beyond

My involvement with the Providence Pals commenced, as nearly as I can recall it, shortly after contributing my first articles to *Crypt of Cthulhu* in 1982, when I met editor Bob Price and S. T. Joshi at Necon 4, held at Rhode Island's Rogers Williams College in the summer of 1983.

There followed a blur of new friendships and a yearly round of Lovecraftian gatherings. Typically we'd celebrate HPL's death in Providence in March, have a birthday celebration in that same city of August, and wind up the year in Marblehead, Massachusetts for Yuletide. There were side excursions to Gloucester, Newburyport, Salem, and Danvers during the early Necronomicon—and even further reaches of darkest Massachusetts. One of the most infamous I recorded for *Crypt* and selected to accompany this brief memoir. That was our accidental brush with the time-honored practice of tomb-robbing while searching for Pickman's studio in Boston's North End.

There were many other highlights. Once, thanks to Dr. Elieen MacNamara's connections, we received a tour of the so-called shunned house and its sidewalk-level basement. On another occasion, we got inside Lovecraft's beloved Ladd Observatory, which inspired my well-received Mythos story, "The Sothis Radiant."

Our finest hour was, without question, the placing of the H. P. Lovecraft memorial plaque on the grounds of the John Hay Library on the occasion of the Lovecraft Centennial Conference in August, 1990. The plaque was the brainchild of Jon B. Cooke, and organized by Jon, S. T. and myself. We pulled off his Mission: Impossible-style fundraising operation in a flat fourteen weeks. Who would have thought such a collection of lost and wayward souls could have conjured up that arcane miracle? But we did.

I don't recall when our gatherings began petering out, but by the mid-1990s, S. T. had moved as far from Providence as inhumanly possible and Bob Price no longer drove up from whatever Deep South hellhole he then inhabited. Marc Michaud was, as I understand it, abducted or was dispossessed by night-gaunts and virtually vanished, Accounts vary. And so, inevitably, we drifted apart.

Others held up the unhallowed torch intermittently, and the Yuletide gatherings continue to be held in Marblehead. I attended one a few years back. But without the old gang, it was like holding a memorial service for a vanished youth in a half-forgotten age.

But all is not dust and ashes. In the summer of 2013, we all once again gathered in Providence for the first bi-annual Necronomicon, sat on panels together, and I sensed an energy I had not felt since attending the First World Fantasy Con in that same city way back in 1975, when its theme as The Lovecraft Circle.

Looking back, I can see that I was privileged to participate in a major resurgence of Lovecraft scholarship that flowered all through the decade of the 1980s and into the 90s. Nothing like it may ever happen again. In our zeal and madness, we lifted every conceivable Lovecraftian rock and sniffed at the disturbing and debatable specimens we uncovered, each one of us discovering different truths, arguing about our wildly varied interpretations, ultimately dispersing like a graduating class that steadfastly refuses to grow up and move on. But move on we did.

Curiously, a number of us, perhaps impelled by scholarly yearnings yet unexpressed, fell into various delusions of all-knowingness. A former Baptist minister, Bob Price now describes himself as a Bible scholar and Christian atheist— whatever that oxymoron may mean. Joshi mutated from a mere materialist into a super-opinionated arch-atheist. Happily, I escaped such extremes, although I will confess to training in spiritual mediumship and coordinate remote viewing and for a time was content live the simple life of a professional psychic.

Well, as a friend once remarked to me, "It's just the Universe universing."

Somewhere in the afterlife, H. P. Lovecraft, his mouth full of celestial ice cream, is chuckling...

FUN GUYS FROM YUGGOTH: WILL MURRAY IN PICKMAN'S FOOTSTEPS

It was probably the ultimate Lovecraftian experience, and it almost didn't happen. But it did happen and –God help me!—I was a witness and unwilling participant in the consecration of Robert M. Price and S. T. Joshi in one of the oldest and most unholy activities practiced by Man since he first began burying his dead.

Friday evening, August 19, 1983. The eve of the anniversary of H. P. Lovecraft's birth and the annual gathering of the New England/New Jersey Lovecraft fan axis in memory of that occasion. Bob Price and S.T. arrived in the early evening. Bob was a bit tuckered from his long drive from Bloomfield, but S.T., whom Bob picked up in Providence, was raring to go. As luck had it, my adventurous companion, Doreen Greeley, arrived just seconds after the others and we were ready for our first Lovecraftian adventure of the weekend.

Inasmuch as the site of the famous "Pickman's Model" was a short drive up the Southeast Expressway from my North Quincy home and none of us had ever prowled that area, I suggested a quick evening jaunt to Boston's North End. Armed with a Lancer edition of THE DUNWICH HORROR and assorted maps, we set off confidently.

And promptly got lost. We'd taken the wrong exit and found ourselves too far north and in the vicinity of Logan Airport, which S.T. was especially displeased to discover, having landed there from England only days before. We doubled back, and again got lost. Well, not *lost* so much as *mislocated* in downtown Boston, which was nice, but not exactly what we had in mind. Bob, fatigued and a trifle nauseous from unexplained causes, began to complain of the latening hour and traffic. We almost turned back at that point, but S.T., perhaps prompted by some unvoiced premonition of what lay ahead, seized the moment and directed Bob in the proper direction. Sort of.

In any case, we soon found ourselves parking on North Street at the edge of one of the endless string of outdoor festivals the Italians hold over the summer in honor of various saints, but which are more like an urban carnival. Bob, S.T., Doreen and I wended our way through the crowds, the food stands and games of chance offering E.T. dolls, under the varicolored bulbs strung in the shape of crowns between the properly crooked streets, in search of Battery Street, the beginning of the trek to the studio of Richard Upton Pickman as described in the story.

Now Lovecraft wrote "Pickman's Model" in the summer of 1926, after a visit to the very part of Boston we were creeping through. He described the immediate neighborhood of Pickman's studio in some detail, dwelling on its sinister alleys and antique houses, but was purposely vague about the exact location of that terrible studio. A year after writing the story, he took Donald Wandrei on a walking tour of the area, and was shocked to discover the precise location of the story had been razed and replaced by brick warehouses. But we were undaunted by this fact because all the streets mentioned by name in the story still existed according to a Boston directory.

We found Battery Street with the help of some natives and in an attempt to find the next step as described in the story, Constitution Wharf, we followed Hanover Street to the waterfront. We never found Constitution Wharf, but as we picked our way between the warehouses, I noticed an alley leading off the landward side of the street. We crossed and found it was Greenough Lane! The narrator of "Pickman's Model" mentions that as he "struck along" Constitution Wharf, he turned up an unnamed street which "wasn't Greenough Lane."

We were on the right track!

The next street was Henchman, a nice sinister street to encounter in the dark. It's mentioned earlier in the story as being the site of one of the "bricked-up arches and wells leading nowhere" which are visible from the elevated train tracks (now a subway, by the way). These openings lead to the network of tunnels where Pickman's ghouls are supposed to dwell. We decided to pass up Henchman Street for the moment and proceeded to the next, named Foster Street.

This street led up a pronounced incline, which I decided held promise. "Let's go up," I suggested. We went up; on the left were various darksome houses and, on the right, what appeared to be brick warehouses or converted apartments. Alleys and cul-de-sacs led off on both sides. There were no "crumbling-looking gables, broken small-paned windows and archaic chimneys" as described by Lovecraft, but these would have been long razed anyway. But the alleys were weird enough.

Now, according to the story, Pickman leads the narrator "to the left into an equally silent and still narrower alley with no light at all; and in a minute made what I think was an obtuse-angled bend toward the right in the dark. Not long after this Pickman produced a flashlight and revealed an antediluvian ten-panelled door that looked damnably worm-eaten."

Alas, we found no such alley, but there was one on the right which was painted yellow and eerily-lit and went off at a right angle to parallel our progress up Foster Street. We passed it by and soon emerged on Charter Street, where the narrator ultimately fled from Pickman's studio. We turned right and found the other end of the right-angled alley. It looked just as eerie at this end.

The entire neighborhood was eerie. We continued along Charter, passing the absolutely black mouths of several alleys. Doreen produced a sealed flashlight from her purse, and what it showed us of those alleys did not invite exploration. A black cat crossed our path at one point (at least, he *looked* black) and the old metal streetlights with their bulbs set in glass cages were obviously from Lovecraft's time. They were irregularly spaced and gave off little light.

We intended to explore any other alleys we chanced to encounter and then double back to look over everything in more detail when we came across the fateful graveyard.

It was plainly an ancient cemetery, fenced off from the street. "This must be Copp's Hill Burying Ground!" I exclaimed. "This is where the ghouls live … and feed." Everyone peered past the wrought-iron bars. Cracked and broken tombstones showed in the near-full moon. Then I found a sign. Except it was *blank*.

"Look, the ghouls have erased the sign!" I cried. For the sign *was* blank, and effaced by large dripping rust patches disquietingly like the pawprints of giant dogs. Or were those *rust* patches? But they were there and we enjoyed the mock-supernatural thrill it gave us.

Wandering around the perimeter of the graveyard, we sought a gate. There was no gate on the Charter Street side, nor at the tower end, where the stone wall holding the graveyard fence rose well above our heads. S.T. and I cautiously put our ears to the wall, expectant of hearing evidence of subterranean activity, but found none.

The gate was around the corner, and to our pleasure, open. Here, Doreen's flashlight really came in handy. As we made our way up the walk, I remarked that I thought I could hear the meeping of ghouls, but decided they were only crickets. "Besides, ghouls meep only in Dreamland. In the real world, they bay." S.T. appreciated the allusion to his latest *Crypt of Cthulhu* article. We heard no baying.

Copp's Hill Burying Ground is a spectral place at ten o'clock at night. It's high enough so we could see the waterfront just down the hill, and to the north. To the east, the white spire of Old North Church loomed. Most of the tombstones dated back to the early 1800s, some as early as 1660, and a few were topped by winged death's-heads. The far end of the yard was blocked off by buildings. We explored it, reading tombstones and joking about what was supposed to lurk under our feet— blissfully unaware of what *really did* lurk beneath the grass.

Doreen discovered it as we were about to leave and called to me. Bob wasn't feeling well, and S.T. and I were hungry. But our pilgrimage to a local pizza parlor was not to be. "Hey, look at this!" I remarked to the others. "It's open!"

It sure was. It was not a head-stone, but one of those obelisk-like shafts used to mark the burial sites of several people. It was similar to the Lovecraft family marker at Swan Point—except that it was *open.*

As we approached to where Doreen was probing the interior with her flash, we could see that one side of the base of the shaft had been worked loose and lay on the ground like a charnel welcome mat. Beyond it was a black hollow.

Being Lovecraft fans and therefore unaccountably drawn to black hollows as a species, we advanced. "Wow! Look—*stairs!*" Doreen called back as we drew near.

We laughed, refusing to believe her. But there they were. Five or six cobwebby stone steps, *and they went in the wrong direction.*

Or, to be more precise, the vandals who had pried open the marker had worked the wrong side loose. We saw the steps coming from the inside of the opposite face and going down. But we couldn't see where they led. We stood on the fallen slab and the steps obviously disappeared somewhere under our feet.

While our imagination worked, S.T. decided that he stood on the threshold of a unique experience. He took the flashlight and entered the shaft. Now here was a brave man. He had read all of Lovecraft and yet did not hesitate to descend into the abyss. Because the steps led in the wrong direction, S.T. had to go down on all fours and back, feet first into the shaft. This he did without incident.

With light filling the interior, S.T. descended. He and Bob thought this an appropriate occasion for a few lines from "The Statement of Randolph Carter."

"Beat it! BEAT IT!" cried S.T. as Bob growled gutterally, "You fool, Joshi is DEAD!"

That brought a laugh, but then S.T. disappeared down the steps. First his head slipped from view then the shaft went dark. He was so far down the backwash of the light was lost! But his voice could still be heard. He was reluctant to describe his discovery in detail when questions were called down, but he was obviously enjoying himself. Bob and I decided to augment his experience by replacing the fallen slab, but it proved too heavy to lift.

Presently, S.T. climbed out, claiming to have seen part of a spinal column. But he wasn't certain. That was too much for Bob, who decided that as editor of *Crypt of Cthulhu*, he was not about to shrink from following in the footsteps of the editor of *Lovecraft Studies*.

Bob experienced some difficulty backing into the interior, which prompted me to misquote Lovecraft: "Do not go downe, what you cannot climb up out of." But he made it, soon disappearing into the depths of the tomb. As S.T. remarked at the time, his bearded face looked especially eldritch in the flashlight glow.

Bob was down there a long, long time, during which the sounds of rummaging through wood could be heard. "Do you hear the sound of *gnawing?*" S.T. asked me at one point. To pass the time, we read the names on the shaft, which were of a husband and wife, who died in their 70s in the early part of the 1900s.

When Bob finally emerged from below, he was grinning like—dare I say it?—a *ghoul.*

"Did you see part of a spinal column down there?" S.T. wanted to know. Then Bob produced a certain brownish-red osseous fragment in wordless confirmation.

I point out that it wasn't wise of Bob to remove such things from a historical burying ground, but he wasn't having any.

I went next. It wasn't hard, although I didn't like the looks of the spiderwebs which dressed the inside of the shaft or the drippings from the stone. But it was awkward. First you had to spot the steps with the light then back into the shaft and drop. There was no way to do this so you could *see* where you were going. It was not for the squeamish.

But once on the steps, the flashlight illuminated everything. Almost. I was amazed at how far the steps went down. At least a dozen feet. I went down the steps, and only when I got near the bottom could I see the crypt. It was possibly eight feet square and ten high. The bottom was littered with various debris among which could be seen two ancient coffins made of planks which had fallen in with age. I didn't see any bones; I didn't much want to see any. It didn't take me long to satisfy my curiosity, and I went back up the stairs, brushing spiderwebs with my hair.

It was Doreen's turn next. Now Doreen is a girl who once told me one of her ambitions is to be the first to discover the body in a famous murder. Doreen declined her turn. But she did find a crack in the shaft which enabled her to see the crypt. That was obviously thrill enough.

By this time S.T. had had time enough to examine Bob's grisly prize. He went back in for one of his own. Sure enough, he came back with a human vertebra identical to Bob's. Bob had also picked up the top of a headstone somewhere. He hastily dropped this when I warned him of approaching people.

Two men with flashlights accosted us at this point, explaining that they were local residents concerned about vandalism in the burying ground and some recent desecrating of graves. He had been about to call the police but, seeing Doreen, came himself. Bob and S.T. put on innocent expressions and hoped the vertebrae in their hands didn't show. I pulled my copy of THE DUNWICH HORROR from a back pocket and began explaining our "Pickman's Model" tour, while Bob and S.T. pocketed their trophies surreptitiously.

To our surprise, the spokesman of the pair, whose name I forget, admitted he was familiar with "Pickman's Model," and began reciting a rough synopsis of the story. It was at this point he dropped a bombshell. In mentioning the tunnels inhabited by Pickman's ghouls, he remarked the local teenagers were in the habit of sneaking down there for drinking parties.

"You mean the tunnels are *real?*"

They were, and they still existed, we were assured. Because we were obviously not up to mischief (ahem) we were given a brief tour of the secret entrance to the tunnel network. There was a false crypt, which had obviously been broken into at one point and restored, and two mock tombs, lacking inscriptions, all of which gave access to the tunnels. The tunnels were a mystery. Some led down to the waterfront, several hundred yards away. One went at right angles from Copp's Hill to the Old North Church, also a good distance away. It was assumed they had been used for smuggling, but no one knew for sure.

"You seem to know a lot about this;" Bob remarked, jumping on an opportunity, "would you be interested in writing an article on this for *Crypt of Cthulhu?*" It turned out that Bob had propositioned a doctor who wrote for medical journals. The latter was taken aback but promised to think about it.

As we parted company under an accusing moon, Bob and S.T. were beside themselves with charnel pleasure.

"Wait'll I tell Lin Carter about this!" Bob exulted. "Wait'll I tell Donna Death!" His nausea, he claimed, had evaporated. S.T. swore the foetid air was responsible.

S.T. fondled his vertebra avidly, muttered his pleasure at having a relic of the 18th century, then expressed his disappointment that he hadn't found a skull down in the crypt. "I really wanted a skull." Some ghouls are never satisfied.

"The dead—" Doreen intoned for possibly the fifth time, quoting Darren McGavin as Carl Kolchak, "do not disturb them for *any* reason."

Later they would tell me that this had been the best Lovecraftian experience in which they'd participated—after all, how many opportunities does one get to become a certified grave-robber? But as we walked away from Copp's Hill Burying Ground, I reflected on how our experience mixed elements of "Pickman's Model", "The Statement of Randolph Carter" and "The Hound." At that thought, I looked up in the sky for signs of winged hounds. Seeing none, I took Doreen's hand.

The next day, we met Jason Eckhardt and his intended, Victoria, in Harvard Square and regaled them with anecdotes of our experience. I suspect they had some difficulty believing all this, but it was entirely true, from the doglike rust prints to the stairs in the crypt. But perhaps the greatest discovery we made came when I prowled through SELECTED LETTERS and found the following in a letter to Earl Peirce dated November 28, 1936:

> I'm interested to know that you've visited the Boston North End section mentioned in "Pickman's Model". This region used to be a good deal more picturesque than it is now, and the sinister alley described in the story was more or less literally based on a real alley (Foster St., I think) which zigzagged peculiarly up from Commercial St. to Charter St. not so very far from Copp's Hill. I'll never forget my mystification when I tried to show this region to Donald Wandrei (whose work in the magazines

you've doubtless read) in 1927, on his first visit to the East. I had been all over it only the year before, and had told Wandrei what curious sights to expect, when lo!—as we approached the district we found only a barren waste of exposed foundations with the line of the former alley traced amidst the wreckage under a blazing sun! The whole damn tangle of alleys had been torn down in the few months between Dec. '26 and June '27, and I had nothing tangible to back up the glowing accounts I had given!

We'd found the correct alley after all! In fact, there is a Foster Court which stems off the left side of Foster Street, and I'll bet that it was the site of Pickman's studio.

Well, it's almost a week later as I write this. Bob and S.T. have departed enwrapped in eldritch exultation. I don't really think they have anything to fear from ghouls or winged hounds. Still, if I were them, I'd be careful. They're liable to hear a rattling knock on their door and find a reddish-brown skeleton with a disquietingly *truncated* spine standing outside ...

BOB KNOX

   Bob Knox was one of the last members to join the "Providence Pals". A Lovecraftian and movie-maniac, Bob would go on to provide the covers for many Necronomicon Press books including the influential *Studies in Weird Fiction* magazine. Bob was also a charitable artist providing many pieces of art for fan projects such as this cover for Ken Neily's EOD zine, *Lovecraftian Ramblings*. Bob remains active in the art scene and has provided many covers to recent publications from several publishers.

–Sam Gafford

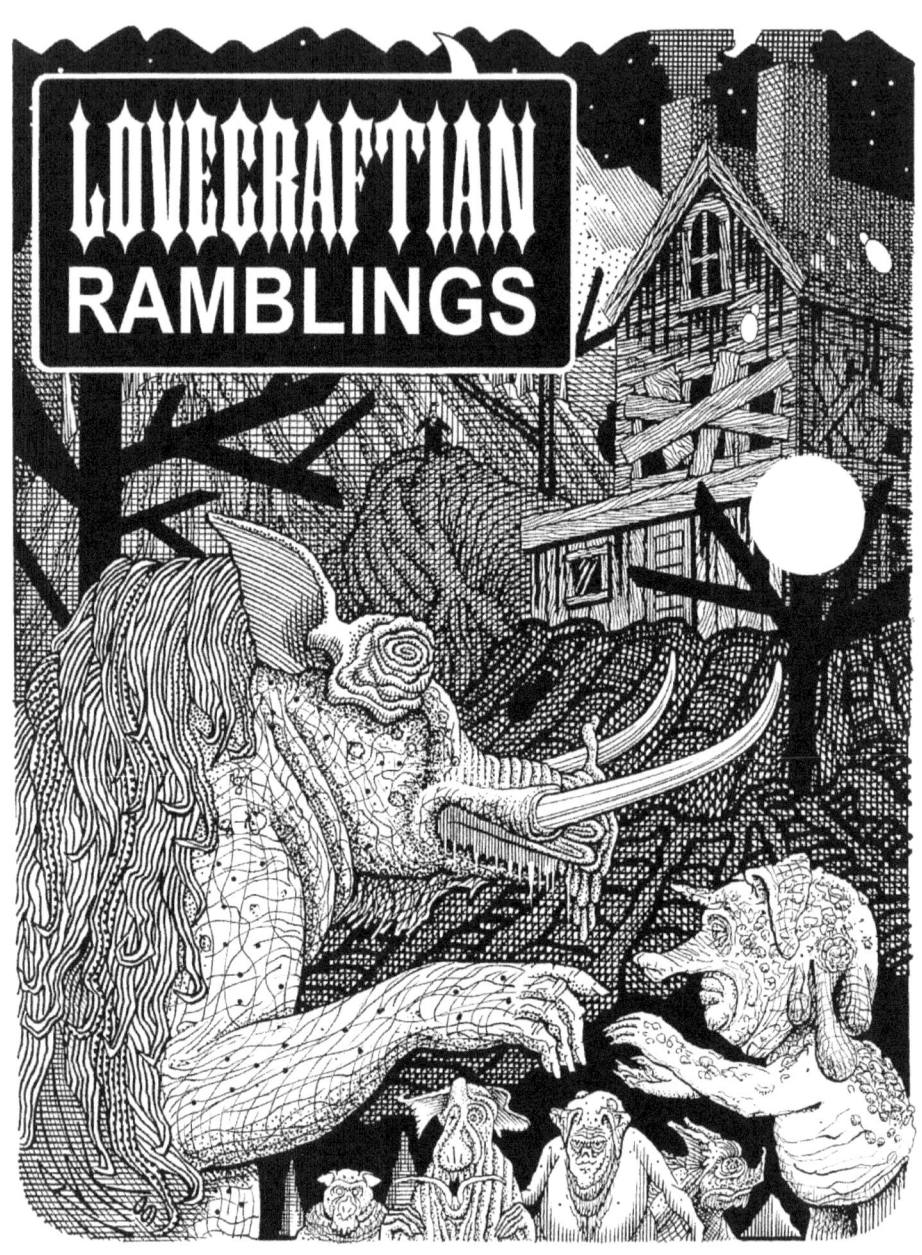

LOVECRAFTIAN RAMBLINGS

KEN NEILY

Ken Neily wasn't a scholar or a writer or an artist or a publisher. What he was was the quintessential *fan*. Ken loved Lovecraft's stories and weird fiction and so many other things that it was hard to keep track of it all. Early on during my time in the Providence Pals, I felt a deep kinship with Ken because we were both, first and foremost, fans. It was easy for me to feel awed by S.T. Joshi, Marc Michaud, Don Burleson and the others but Ken was like an older big brother and we spend a lot of time talking about Lovecraft and weird fiction and old television shows and obscure movies and so many other things. Ken was one of the first people to clue me in about the work of William Hope Hodgson which would become a later passion in my life. Whenever we'd meet, he'd regale me with his new collecting obsession and we'd laugh and talk about new things we'd added to our collections.

Ken passed away last year in 2014 after a long illness and a stroke. Some of the Providence Pals were able to get up there and say "goodbye" and "thank you" before he passed. I wish I'd gotten this project done in time for him to see this because it's the kind of thing that he'd look it, smile and say, in that certain way of his, "well, gawddamn, look at that."

He wasn't a scholar or a writer or an artist or a publisher but he was one of us. He was and always will be a Providence Pal.

--Sam Gafford

(Note: The cartoons of Ken that follow were drawn by Bob Knox and appeared in Ken's EOD fanzine, LOVECRAFTIAN RAMBLINGS.)

The Fart Side

Uncle K'noth-Nyloth as a child

The Fart Side

As Murphy would have it, the Bomb was dropped on
Sanbornville just as Channel 6 was about to show
the Lost Episode of "Magnum, P. I.".

The Fart Side

"They were usually feeding—
I won't say on what."

-Pickman's Model

cabin~fever.

www.ingramcontent.com/pod-product-compliance
Lightning Source LLC
Chambersburg PA
CBHW060128260626
47160CB00005B/2049